Fred van Zuiden

CALL ME MOM

T° CHERYL

NEVER AGAIN

CALL ME MOM

Fred van Zuiden

CALL ME MOM

A Dutch Boy's WW II Survival Story

By
Fred van Zuiden

Fourteenth printing May 2013

Published by:
G.B. Batteries Ltd.
#609, 3339 Rideau Place SW
Calgary, AB, Canada T2S 1Z5

Email: vanzuiden@agt.net
www.callmemom.ca
Editor: Pat Kozak
Layout & Design: By Design Desktop Publishing Inc. Principal: Sue Impey
Cover: By Design Desktop Publishing Inc. Principal: Sue Impey

Printed and bound in Canada by BlitzPrint

Library and Archives Canada Cataloguing in Publication

Van Zuiden, Fred, 1930-
    Call me Mom : a Dutch boy's WW II survival story / Fred van Zuiden ; editor: Pat Kozak.

Includes bibliographical references.
ISBN 978-0-9736870-2-6
eISBN 978-0-9736870-3-3

    1. Van Zuiden, Fred, 1930- --Childhood and youth.
2. Hidden children (Holocaust)--Netherlands--Biography.
3. Jews--Netherlands--Biography. 4. Netherlands--History--German occupation, 1940-1945--Biography. 5. World War, 1939-1945--Personal narratives, Dutch. 6. Netherlands--Biography. I. Kozak, Pat II. Title.

DS135.N6V365 2009   940.53'18092   C2009-901218-9

I dedicate my words to the Hollanders brave enough to hide and protect the persecuted during the Occupation, to those who lost their lives pursuing freedom, and to the memory of Karel (Carl) Keuning

By the same author:

The Sailing Game: Life in the Sailboat World

CONTENTS

PROLOGUE

With a thunderous crash, my father's fist hit the table. He pushed his plate away, shoved his chair back, and stormed out of the dining room. Pieces of rare roast beef lay splattered over the tablecloth like bodies on a blood-soaked battle field.

At nine years old I was aware of the frightening rumbles of war. I always grabbed the newspaper first and saw shots of the Japanese butchering people in Nanking, and Mussolini's tanks slaughtering horse-borne Abyssinians. These awful photos deeply affected me. In Germany, brown-shirted Nazi bullies were burning books, vandalizing synagogues, and smashing storefronts. My young heart pounded as I read about this terrible violence. The Civil War in Spain also alarmed me, even though I did not really know what a civil war was.

My father was growing alarmed, too, and was constantly telling my mother we should leave Holland. We were a Jewish family, and he knew we would be in danger if the Germans occupied our country. Father harped on and on about going to America. Mother usually reacted badly, her bosom heaving as she broke into tears and screamed, "No, no, no, Marius!"

I can see her now in her fashionable polka-dot red dress raging that Holland was no more going to war now than it did twenty-five years ago. She had no doubt whatsoever that her high-society life would continue, and she seemed oblivious to the threat to our borders.

Finally Father lost patience; scenes became a regular occurrence at mealtimes. Along with my brother and sister, fourteen-year-old Arjay and four-year-old Annemie, I sat stunned through these tirades. There was no doubt my sympathies were with Father; my mother's tears didn't move me one bit. I was taking those frightening newspaper photos very seriously and would have jumped at the chance to escape to America.

Day by day there were more alarming events. In February 1938 Germany annexed Austria with ninety percent of the Austrians welcoming the takeover by the native born Hitler. Next, bold as brass, the Germans took over part of Czechoslovakia.

War was officially declared by the English and French on September 4th, 1939, when Germany attacked Poland, but it had no immediate effect on Holland. From then on I left for school early each day so I could study the map of Poland in the window of a local store. The western front line was changing fast. The Germans were using new invasion tactics, including forcing their infantry to march up to a relentless fifty-five kilometres a day. The aggressors mercilessly bombed Poland with their Stuka bombers; the shrieking noise from these diving planes scared the daylights out of everyone below.

Russia, then a German ally, attacked Poland from the east, and the two armies destroyed Poland in a mere three weeks. This new lightning form of warfare immediately became known as *Blitzkrieg* and it wrought unheard of destruction.

Despite the German victories, my childish innocence and patriotism convinced me our strong military could resist any attack on the Netherlands. One of my young friends was very scared of an invasion. I comforted him by cockily insisting we could not be defeated. My naive confidence would soon be crushed.

CHAPTER 1

THE ROOF CAVES IN

I was in Amersfoort staying with my favourite aunt and uncle, Eva and Willem de Vries, when the Germans invaded our country. It was May 10th, 1940.

It so happened that my parents were on holiday close by. Father cycled four kilometres across town to bring us the news. He pounded on the front door and kept his finger on the bell. Aunt Eva, scared from the commotion, got up quickly and pushed the door release. We had been around the table chatting away over our large Dutch breakfast, blissfully unaware of the invasion. In an instant we were silent, frozen by the insistent bell. Father came storming up, leaping two steps at a time over the sedate Persian carpet. White faced, he bellowed, "At three this morning the Germans invaded. We must leave immediately for the Overveen house; we will be safer there!"

Breakfast was forgotten. My cousins and I frantically asked a thousand questions but nobody took any notice of us.

And so began five years of tragedy.

The adults already knew in their guts what was in store for us. Aunt Eva hysterically grabbed Dad's arm shrieking, "Marius dear, what is coming, what is coming?" She got in his way as he attempted to make departure plans with Uncle Willem, and he roughly told her to sit down and keep quiet. I was to go with my parents and Annemie on bicycles, and Uncle Willem would leave by car with Aunt Eva and my two cousins. My brother Arjay would travel with other relatives. While father was rattling out his instructions, the maid walked in and calmly cleared the table.

We began preparations to flee to the sanctuary of the Overveen house that same day. Father and his brother Gerard had bought this house when they feared war was inevitable; he felt Overveen would be safer than our hometown, Hoogeveen, because it was behind the water defence line. Unimaginably, father had agreed to three more of his brothers and their families joining us. Along with the de Vries family, that would make nineteen people.

When Uncle Willem's car left, it was jammed so full with clothes and food the passengers could hardly be seen. While we assembled our bikes for the journey, Father muttered over and over, "I was stupid not to have learned to drive." Mother was just plain bitching.

Father had the added burden of carrying Annemie in the little child seat on the crossbar. She was probably sleepy because she wasn't squawking, which she usually did. We kids had helped Mother make smelly boiled egg sandwiches, which we now stuffed in our lunch boxes. Father strapped our small suitcases to the bike racks.

Overveen was about seventy kilometres away; our solemn little cycling group set out to tackle this demanding distance. My conniving brother wriggled his way into riding in a car with Uncle Phili. For once Arjay didn't complain, even though the car was loaded to the hilt and the passengers were squashed in amongst the provisions.

At the outset I was excited by our evacuation plan and considered it high adventure, but by the time we had gone ten kilometres I was tired from the exertion and drained by the excitement. "Are we nearly there?" I asked repeatedly.

Father put on a brave face but I saw he was worried out of his mind about our safety. Before we set out, we heard that the invading troops had already reached Hoogeveen. He was also concerned about the business and his employees. Dad and I talked over everything. I was only nine years old, so I was surprised he was taking me into his confidence. I guess he was trying to get things off his chest without worrying Mother. I suddenly felt grown up.

Our route was the same one we had travelled numerous times when one of the uncles drove us to beach resorts. Covering this distance on my bike was a new experience and I was finding it very hard. I continually felt like crying and was no longer thinking of high adventures. Baby sister Annemie had already fallen sound asleep.

Our expedition gave the first smell of what war was going to mean. The route was not yet occupied but we did see Dutch soldiers on guard outside important government buildings. There was constant gunfire in the distance and Father explained it was from anti-aircraft installations. He speculated the Germans would target our air bases, the Government and Royal Palaces, along with the Hilversum radio stations.

Shortly after, a low-flying German twin engine plane roared overhead. We were petrified. We saw its black iron cross and swastika, our first experience of these terrifying enemy icons. "It's a Junker 52," I shouted as soon as I could speak again, proud that I had been able to identify the aircraft.

We pedalled on through the low-lying terrain. Father tried to cheer us up by telling us we would take a break in Amsterdam. It had been hard going, but the terrain was now flatter. The familiar fields and hundreds of cows had a calming effect on my parents, and this trickled down to me. None of us had had any practice for this mammoth cycle trip and all the pedalling exhausted us. I couldn't help wondering if we would reach the Overveen house that night.

Our few minutes of calm abruptly ended when we were confronted by a Dutch military road block. This was something new and something else to scare us. The block was formed by concrete pillars and upturned trucks. Father produced identification and our hearts pounded, but the soldiers waved us through. I could see my father relax as we intrepid cyclists went on our way.

"My legs are going numb with all the pedalling," I whined, thoroughly irritable and starving. Mother agreed we would stop at the next roadside table. We didn't sit for long, just enough time to gobble down our lunches and stretch our legs. I was hardly aware I was pedalling again but Father helped by keeping his hand on my back and pushing me. This was no mean feat considering he had to keep his own balance with Annemie on his bike. Despite everyone's fatigue we ate up the kilometres; by late afternoon we reached Amsterdam.

We made our way over the uneven cobblestoned streets looking for Uncle Sam. Sam was Father's favourite brother, so we knew we would get a good rest and a meal. With my last strength I struggled to keep my bike upright. When we arrived, Father had to carry me up the stairs to the second-floor apartment. Sam, Greta and their two girls hugged each of us in turn then they fed us a wonderful meal of eggs and sausages on toast.

The food fortified us, but did not lift our spirits. Both families were glum, afraid we would be bombed at any minute. After eating, we trooped downstairs and went outside to stare at the sky. We were looking for enemy planes. Perhaps the adults thought that looking would scare off German attacks. Uncle Sam was extremely jittery and Father, full of his usual goodwill, agreed that Sam and his family should join our Overveen house contingent. "Father, that's twenty three people!" I gasped. No one seemed to hear me. Sam's mood changed from glum to pure joy. The family packed their belongings in a wink.

Taxis were scarce but they had one organized quickly. It was only thirty kilometres to Overveen, but I was upset that Father had not arranged for Annemie and me to finish the journey in the taxi. I was thoroughly put out when our cousins cheerily waved goodbye as they passed us mounting our bikes. We never caught up with the taxi, but we did reach our Overveen hideaway on Brazil Lane at eight that evening. We were completely exhausted, but thrilled to be in one piece. We suddenly thought of the trip in terms of survival. Thankfully, the weather had been warm and sunny during the entire journey; I know we would not have made it in rain or wind.

Mother had been generally silent throughout the trip, often breaking into tears. Now almost hysterically she kept repeating, "God will protect us all." Father, on other hand, just discussed all his worries with each family member in turn. When he was alone, he kept repeating, "Twenty-three people, twenty-three people!"

There were seven bedrooms and two bathrooms at the house, and we van Zuidens were given a top floor room. Uncle Gerard told us the families had been arriving since two o'clock. We had been the last to get there. The ladies had organized themselves and food was coming out of the kitchen. The dining table was extended to accommodate twelve and the kitchen table was set, too, so we all managed to eat at the same time.

My admiration for Father's foresight in acquiring the Brazil Lane property knew no bounds. The house was comfortably furnished and the provisions stored in the basement easily stretched to the six families. I couldn't grasp how he had planned for nineteen people, never mind twenty-three. He had been mobilized into the army reserve during the previous Great War, so he must have learned this organizational talent during his service. Each time I saw his reserve rifle standing in the corner of the parental bedroom I giggled, but now I knew better. He once told me he didn't have the heart to throw it out.

We needed to shop and I went with Uncle Willem and Aunt Eva in the Dodge. Willem's first worry was to fill up with gas at Mr. Bloemendaal's garage. The owner had already started rationing and Willem could get only twenty litres, but there was no price gouging or any sign of black-marketeering.

We next stopped at a grocery store and were happily surprised to find plenty of food on the shelves. We bought a good supply of bread and fresh items. The ladies in the household marvelled at the staples in the basement alongside the dried meat, sausages, eggs and mounds of cans. The house had good running water and the families had arrived with more food, so lack of nourishment was not one of our worries.

The aunts thought us children should understand the gravity of our situation, so they called us in to do the menial tasks, such as peeling potatoes and cleaning. They even persuaded Arjay to help out.

Generally, mealtimes were lively gatherings and the aunts soon found several sittings were easier than all trying to eat at once. We had the radio on during meals and listened anxiously trying to digest the war news still broadcasting from Radio Hilversum. We learned the Royal Family and Government ministers had fled the country by boat from Ijmuiden, which was only a few kilometres from us. After I heard this, I wondered why we didn't try to get on one of the boats bound for Britain. Other people had this great idea, but most who tried were refused at the docks. I can only imagine the drama of families packing for an escape and their disappointment at having to go home.

Despite the situation, there were many light moments at Brazil Lane during those first uncertain days after the invasion. A Dutch army officer and his wife were living across the road, and for some unknown reason he was at home. They had left the curtains wide open and we could see the officer embracing his wife again and again. We kids giggled but Uncle Sam explained the officer needed to get back to his unit and was probably making the most of the last few minutes with his wife.

Right from the start the Dutch military fought valiantly but some of the soldiers and officers suffered from fear and shell shock once under battle conditions. Several in this group were persuaded at gunpoint to leave the safety of their underground trenches to face the fierce fighting.

The Dutch Government planned to flood parts of Holland in the event the Germans invaded. The Overveen house was on land behind the flood line and thus sat in a safe haven. Our sense of security was shattered when we learned that our waterline safety net had disappeared into thin air. The Government's plans to flood the area came to naught because the Germans ignored the line by going round it or flying over it.

On the second day after the invasion we learned the German paratroopers and gliders who had landed north of The Hague were now only twenty kilometres away from us. On the third day, the radio broadcast that French troops had come to Holland's aid in the southwest and both Dutch and French were giving the Germans fierce resistance. On the fourth day, the Luftwaffe bombed our port city of Rotterdam and hundreds of civilians were killed. On the fifth day, the Netherlands surrendered.

My youthful faith in the Dutch army fizzled, but I was proud that our soldiers put up five days of fierce resistance. If there had not been a vicious blackmail threat to bomb Amsterdam, Utrecht and The Hague in the same way Rotterdam had been levelled, the fighting might have continued. The Dutch were incensed by the flattening of Rotterdam and the annihilation of its people, and we could not allow more of such destruction. And so surrender came about.

After the capitulation, the Overveen house was useless. Our family suffered the indignity of watching German armoured personnel carriers sweep into Overveen a mere one day after the surrender. We couldn't believe our eyes as these invincible gods of war sat ramrod straight, their ugly helmets resting on their shoulders as if they had no necks, their rifles at the ready. Angst and awe gripped our cores. Our lives altered in an instant, or as the Savant, Father Cats would say, "How times can change." Indeed, these same German soldiers would be decimated only two years later in the Russian battle for Stalingrad.

Within weeks, Hitler appointed an Austrian Nazi, Seyss-Inquart, as Commissioner of the Netherlands and our lives changed for the worse. This individual was to become a ruthless, dictatorial animal bent on pleasing Hitler.

Our Brazil Lane sojourn came to an end. The various relatives departed for their homes, but not without another crisis. During the last five momentous days my mother had become seriously ill, and was much too sick to travel home. Mother's sister, Nell, stayed behind to look after her.

My mother's condition declined every day, so Nell called Father back to Brazil Lane to deal with the frightening situation. We had all felt the strain of fleeing from home, but Mother's dilettante life had in no way prepared her for the rigours of the journey. We began to wonder if she was ailing from something more serious. When Father and Uncle Willem saw her, they decided she needed professional medical help. They carried her to the car and made her comfortable with numerous blankets. Uncle Willem drove directly to Haarlem General Hospital. Saying little, they sat for hours waiting for the doctor to give Father the diagnosis.

The news was bad; she had advanced leukemia and was in very poor shape. When Father came home and told us, he almost broke down. He managed to hug me but quickly fell silent. I think he had been expecting the worse, but even so was in a state of shock.

In the silence, I started thinking about my fun-loving Mother. The invasion had affected her more than any of us because she had so stoutly maintained war would never come. Also, I'm sure, her guilt at thwarting Dad's emigration plans weighed heavily on her mind. It was all too much for her. Despite receiving blood from Aunt Nell, Mother could not fight the leukemia.

After five weeks at the Haarlem hospital, Sientje van Zuiden died on June 17th. Father brought her to our hometown for burial. His face was a gut-wrenching sight during the funeral and my little sister cried the whole time. Arjay and I were shaken to the core. Although we generally did not get on well, Arjay confided to me that he thought even if mother had been well, she probably would not have been able to cope with what the occupation might bring.

Commentary

The Dutch military had failed to grasp or take seriously the new warfare mode of lightning aerial infantry attacks that had been used effectively in the thirties. The generals justified their outmoded tactics by claiming Holland's watery landscape conditions were quite different. No one envisioned Germany attacking Holland, Belgium, Luxembourg and France in one swoop.

Military historians attacked Holland's claim that watery landscapes were not compatible with airborne landings. They were right. In fact, water made no difference; the Germans merely flew over it and landed their paratroopers and gliders at their targeted spots in Western Holland. What could not be disputed was the fierce Dutch opposition; our soldiers were able to destroy at least 200 German planes, mainly Junkers, and incapacitate or kill some 2,000 German paratroopers.

The impact of how fast German troops moved was brought home to me when I saw an old black and white photo. After a mere two hours of invading our country, a group of German infantry in full battle dress were posing in front of my grandmother's house, as they passed through town.

Despite the heavy bombardment, the Dutch Marines and Navy in Rotterdam, prior to the armistice, refused to lay down their arms and forever enhanced their reputation. Additionally, the Dutch were gratified to learn their destruction of the 200 enemy planes during the initial invasion impeded the Germans from making an efficient assault on Crete in 1941. A few sweet moments came from the awful losses.

CHAPTER 2

PRE-WAR FAMILY LIFE

After my mother died, I thought a lot about my parents and about our family life. Mother was from a well-to-do family in our canal-dominated community. Her parents disliked Marius van Zuiden from the start and put up enormous opposition to the marriage. However, young love won out, and a marriage took place. Even after we three kids were born, the intense dislike between Father and his in-laws never went away and it caused friction between my parents.

Father was the youngest of seven children from an industrious merchant family that had been in northeast Holland for at least one hundred and seventy years. He was proud of his ancestors and often told me how resilient they were. They sold textiles and did well, despite the fact their carts often slid in the ditches on the damp, peat-laced soil. "They merely hauled themselves out, brushed themselves off, and sold the goods at attractive discounts, whether wet or dry," Father would say with a smile. "I like to keep my stock moving too."

Later generations built stores, which prospered over the years. The van Zuidens became a respected family with a good standing in the community. Father's reputation was enhanced when he rescued twins from a baby carriage that had rolled into a deep canal. While others stood by he jumped in to the rescue. He loved showing off the bravery medal presented to him by Queen Emma, and he wore it proudly for the rest of his life.

Eventually Father took over the growing textile business. His natural acumen paid off and by 1928 he had built it into a large department store. It was a gigantic undertaking for that time, and although there was no hint of the coming world depression, he managed to keep his store prospering when that dark period hit Holland. By 1939 the bustling business had about twenty-five employees.

Even though we kids caught the fallout from our parent's imperfect marriage, I had an unruffled, if not particularly happy childhood. I continually craved more of my father's attention and was in seventh heaven when he tossed me in the air or gave me bear hugs. He was mostly too busy to play with us kids, plus he travelled a lot. Mother did not spend much time with us, either. In fact, housekeepers and nannies gave us more attention than she did. To me, it seemed as though she was always out with her friends or entertaining in the front parlour.

The girls who did the alterations realized my parents' shortcomings and I gave no resistance when they took me under their collective wing. They dressed me up as a girl to show off my long, black curls and spoilt me rotten with numerous childish delights. Although I enjoyed it, I was seriously embarrassed by all the extra attention. Father knew the girls wasted time playing with me and he or his brother were always galloping up the stairs to pull me out of the sewing room. In panic, I would dive under the sewing machines.

Growing up in that bustling store was fun, even though our antics got us into trouble sometimes. Arjay, our cousin Ben and I created havoc playing hide-and-seek between the long rows of clothing in the showrooms and knocking everything awry. Father and the managers went mad over these disruptions and the atmosphere reached fever pitch as they chased us with broomsticks. Sometimes I was forced to stay hiding for so long I would have to pee in my shoe.

By the time I was eight, the older cousins and Arjay were experimenting with cigarettes in the furnace room, the danger of fire never entering their heads. I gave smoking a try but was sicker than a dog when I inhaled the first time. I was really put off cigarettes.

Several of our cousins used to come and stay with us during the summer holidays and Ben and Arjay would skulk off to the furnace room for a forbidden smoke. Bram and I kept quiet about their antics, but I smelled more smoke than usual one day and I just knew their tossed cigarette butts were smouldering. My mother smelled smoke, too, and had already called the fire brigade. She rushed to the furnace room yelling, "The entire store and living quarters are blue with smoke!" The firemen came lumbering down pulling hoses, and we helped with water pails. The fire was soon under control but I was already worried Father would be angry with me.

When he finally came home from walking his Belgian Shepherd, Mom rushed at him with the horrific details of the fire brigade visit. Father quickly unleashed his wrath, particularly on innocent Bram. I had a quick lesson that injustice often starts at home.

The month of December was always a busy, happy time in our store. The Dutch heavily celebrated the age-old Saint Nicholaas Feast on the fifth day, visiting family and exchanging gifts. The mythical Saint Nick rode his white stallion over the roof tops with the Negro Black Peter at his side. The two dropped gifts down all the chimneys and the children in the household left pumpernickel, water and straw for the travellers.

Our store, which was called The Sun, was famous far and wide for its annual Saint Nicholaas gift promotions. Families crowded outside waiting for the doors to open. All the kids had been on their best behaviour so they could tell Saint Nick on his throne how good they were.

My first big disillusionment in life came in my fifth year. I wandered into the changing room where the saint and his helper were dressing for the promotion. I saw Saint Nick hanging a white beard on his ears and caught Black Peter with only half his face painted. They shooed me out of the room in a flash, but I had already seen too much. I didn't tell my parents of the revelation, fearing my gifts might stop coming down the chimney.

As well as seeing us during the Saint Nicholaas celebrations, Father's large family often went on holidays with us in the summer. We went to beaches and lakes in the north. I became a regular fish leaping in and out of the water all day and also learned to sail and play tennis.

Occasionally, we went to Knocke in Belgium, and I saw myself as a world traveller. I would sneak away and stroll down wide boulevards enjoying the smell of mussels, fries and suntan lotions. I became mad with desire to ride the brightly coloured pedal cars. These were happy, sunny times, but day-to-day life was not always so pleasant.

The daily tension in my parent's marriage made me uneasy. Father's rift with his in-laws grew worse as the years passed, so that didn't help. The success of The Sun and Father's role as a director of a huge buying cooperative meant he did not spend much time at home. Mother made little effort to understand the demands on him and she rarely helped in the store.

Father was smart enough to see that this unsettled family life was affecting me. I was nervous and irritable and had developed a bad temper. He sent me on frequent visits to Amersfoort to stay with my Uncle Willem and Aunt Eva. It became my second home. Amersfoort, which was only few hours away from my home, was a sophisticated, ancient city with many attractions for my enquiring mind.

I was welcomed as a son and little brother. The de Vries family lavished me with love and attention and my demeanour improved greatly. My cousins Meta and Henny were in their mid twenties. Even though they were both busy studying for their doctorates, they devoted time to helping me upgrade my arithmetic and English. I was shocked to find my education was not up to big-city standards. I was keen to improve my knowledge because I hoped to work in Uncle Willem's flourishing hardware distribution business one day.

Henny and Meta also helped improve my social skills. Up till then I hadn't realized such skills existed; I am quite sure it never occurred to my parents to teach us how to behave in polite society.

They made me sit up straight at the table by putting books under my arms. Such indignities! However, I learned to tolerate their nagging and teasing and no longer got angry when Henny and Meta scorned my provincial ways. I was soaking up the lessons, knowing I needed them.

I turned nine while staying in Amersfoort and I was having the time of my life. Uncle Willem took me on business trips, too, and I was thrilled to be riding around in his luxurious American automobile. This was a special treat for me because Father did not have a car. He felt that it would be pretentious to have a vehicle in our small hometown. I am sure Uncle Willem secretly enjoyed driving me around. He explained how business worked and we often called in at humming manufacturing plants and foundries. In awe, I watched molten steel being poured. I began to understand Holland's geography and fast became a very proficient map reader.

This happy state of affairs was not to last, of course. The great change in our lives occurred on May 10th, 1940. Two days earlier, Aunt Eva, claiming she had special powers, predicted war would come. The rest of us felt she was a little nutty and was merely trying to create a mysterious aura around herself. When her daughters could get a word in, they yelled in unison, "You are an eternal pessimist, Mom."

Despite the fact many Hollanders refused to believe war was imminent, there had been hints of war for some time. One such incident occurred in

1939 when 300 German Jewish children arrived in our hometown en route to England. Father was told their parents had paid the German government to let their children leave the country. This usually unemotional man bustled around to arrange for food and blankets to be delivered to the kids.

There were also signs of increased anti-Semitism. In our hometown, young Jewish lads were having their pants pulled down by bullies to reveal their circumcised penises. Anti-Jewish propaganda was spreading its tentacles deeper into all walks of Dutch life. For no rational reason, some local people engaged in persecution of Jews who had been their neighbours for years. My hometown was considered a strong Christian community, yet persecution was found in many corners.

Commentary

Two of my relatives, cousin Brad and his wife Greetje, were secretly flown out of Holland to England in 1941. It was a miraculous escape in an amphibious plane out of our tightly occupied country. Once in England, Greetje became a nurse and Brad joined the Dutch Princess Irene Brigade. He fought in Normandy, France and Belgium. He came through the fighting relatively unscathed until bad luck caught him when he stepped on a landmine. He died after clinging to life for nine days.

Bram, the cousin who had caught flack over the smoking incident when we were kids, immigrated to Israel. The last time I saw him, he was still complaining about the bad rap he got from my father!

CHAPTER 3

THE BULLIES TAKE OVER

After Mother's funeral, Aunt Fie took over our motherless household along with maintaining her own family of three next door. I suspected this arrangement would not last long when I saw her more irritable as each day passed. Caring for the two families was probably beyond anyone's capacity.

Uncle and Aunt de Vries stepped into the breach again and took over my care. Father really loved his sister Eva and it was lucky our two families had such a good relationship. There was a minimum of time wasted on the negotiations, and in a flash I was back in the Amersfoort house. I was really excited about returning and thought it the best thing to happen to me. I happily slipped into the new school and Meta and Henny resumed their extra tutoring and polishing of my provincial manners. Back home, Father employed a series of housekeepers to look after Arjay and Annemie.

Although I had spent many holidays in Amersfoort, I suffered culture shock learning to live in what was to me a large city. Amersfoort, which had thrived since the Middle Ages, had a permanent population of 52,000 by 1940. It was a major rail and highway hub and on the direct route to all major Dutch cities. The city housed a garrison for about 30,000 troops along with a large military hospital.

Although Holland was now under a state of war, life still continued its usual path for most people. I swam and dived to my heart's content in

Amersfoort's numerous canals, even though some of them were plugged with military obstacles. The huge ice age boulder in the city centre absolutely fascinated me. I got to know my new hometown intimately and I wondered if I should become a tourist guide when I grew up.

After the invasion, the Germans quickly housed some 50,000 of their own soldiers in Amersfoort's forbidding stone barracks. On my rambles I saw the German soldiers being intensively trained in the swimming pools and speculated this was in anticipation of an assault on England's south coast. I stood watching men jump off high boards and supposed they either sank or learned to swim fast.

To instil fear into the Dutch population the German troops were frequently paraded arrogantly through the centre of Amersfoort, scraping their metal soled boots on the road surface, all the time singing loudly, "We are sailing to England." Our people feared and hated these displays but managed to laugh when they saw the children cheekily mimic torpedoed Germans in the water.

I also explored the countryside surrounding Amersfoort, and the wild beauty of the woods and villages quickly seduced me. Sometimes I would drag a friend along; we would cycle to the woods and play for hours. I was awe struck when I discovered the fast-flowing and wide rivers named Rhine, Waal and Maas, and watched all the barge commerce. It did not occur to me that rivers were major obstacles in times of war.

As much as I was thrilled by my new big city school, I was highly embarrassed to learn that my small-town grade 4 standards were not good enough to pass into the next class. The headmaster told Uncle Willem I was a year behind, so he made the girls coach me even harder. My days of freedom exploring the town and countryside came to an end, and suddenly I was immersed in study. I worked every evening till bedtime and was really miserable when Uncle insisted I work weekends too. When the neighbourhood kids invited me to play, I had to turn them away.

But extra study soon became the least of my worries. I suffered a jolt when Dutch Nazism entered my school. We all had little desks, and I could see the boy in front of me continually drawing planes with swastikas plastered all over them, which he then tossed around the classroom. He was a noisy boy and kept proclaiming the Germans would bomb England to pieces and he couldn't wait for the bombing to start. The boy's father owned a local railway bar and probably had already become a member of the Dutch Nazi Party or an *NSBayer*

(Nationaal-Socialistische Beweging) as we called them. He had indoctrinated his son well and I wondered if he would enrol the boy in the Dutch version of the Hitler Youth group.

Despite the setbacks my new school was stimulating my brain. I became capable of almost instantaneous calculation and was doing well in the basics of the French and English languages. I was always athletic and now I became a gymnast and rope climber. The baseball team recruited me and it was soon my favourite game. I roller skated three kilometres to and from school most days and became fitter than ever I had been. I could easily walk ten kilometres.

I might have been enjoying a normal life but living in occupied Holland became a little more unpleasant every day, particularly so for Jewish families. We found out what the rumoured Nuremberg laws were to mean to our daily lives. It only took fourteen days after the invasion for the first edicts to be implemented. Month after month new and harsher laws were promulgated. Uncle and Aunt became more worried every day and my confidence ebbed.

One demand was for Jewish households to deliver their radios to the German military authority. They wanted to keep us in the dark about the war news as well as the vicious propaganda being aimed at the Jews and other unloved minorities. Keeping us without knowledge was just another means of ratcheting up our terror. It worked well. The occupiers tried their best to prevent the Dutch from listening to news from the free world being broadcast by Radio Orange out of facilities set up in London's BBC. This was the only source of factual news, but it was illegal for any Dutch person to receive it. Pretty quickly a hidden radio network was formed, which included France's *Ici Londres* station and Belgium's cheeky station called something like, *We will smash the Jerries, with or without luck!*

With all my concentrated schooling I had a pretty good memory so I was sent every day to a neighbour who had a hidden radio. I was very proud of this responsibility and listened intently to the six o'clock Radio Orange news broadcast and then ran the one block home to report the details.

Everyone was hungry for news from the outside world, even though it was mostly bad. I trained myself to absorb the whole broadcast and would then rush home and make an almost verbatim report. There was news from myriad fronts. Battles were raging in North Africa, the North Atlantic and the Pacific, and all of it tumbled out of my throat.

In1941, after the German invasion of Russia and the Japanese attack on Pearl Harbour, my news reports became even more detailed. It was an exciting time when the Americans declared war on the Axis powers of Japan, Germany and Italy. Finally we had a whiff of the tide turning. The more I reported the more expert I became about the news. We all lived through the horrors I described about the fall of Hong Kong and the overrunning of the Philippines, Dutch East Indies and Singapore.

I experienced a tingling sensation while passing on the hope-inspiring speeches of Churchill, Roosevelt, Stalin and Queen Wilhelmina, and I prided myself that I remembered the orations almost word for word.

The deterioration of Amersfoort life picked up as more and more war measures entered our lives. One summer afternoon in 1941 I saw hundreds of emaciated Russian and Ukrainian prisoners being herded through the city centre. Earlier that day at the station siding I had watched these same prisoners tumbling out of cattle cars. Most of them immediately dropped to their knees and frantically tried to eat the grass along the platform. I was sure they had not been fed for days. The guards mercilessly prodded and screamed at the men to keep moving along the road. That scene suddenly made me understand the Germans really did consider some of their fellow men sub-human.

These highly effective methods to dehumanize people were being employed against prisoners as well as the Jewish population. I walked alongside the marching prisoners and watched while the poor wretches were herded towards the Amersfoort concentration camp. I knew most of them would perish quickly. It was the first time I had seen cattle cars used to transport human beings.

A friend of Uncle Willem's found a swastika painted on the tiles in front of his high-end fashion store in the main square. He was in the process of scrubbing it clean when a passing Dutch Nazi arrested him on the spot. A van arrived quickly and Uncle's friend was taken to the same Amersfoort concentration camp.

This mild, gentle friend was abused and beaten to such an extent that he died a few days later. Thousands of pitiable victims from all levels of Dutch society would die cruelly, guilty of minor infractions blown out of all proportion.

Most Hollanders found it disturbing to live under the new occupation laws and were appalled at the treatment singled out against the Jews and gypsies. The seemingly inconsequential rules and regulations changed almost daily and became harder and harder to tolerate.

The Dutch took pride in their administrative perfection but it was flung back in their face. The Nazis checked municipal records and easily picked out Jewish families, obliging them to wear the yellow star. I saw so many stars out on the streets I knew German efficiency was getting the upper hand. Initially our family refused to wear the identifying sign, but when Uncle found out adults and even children were being imprisoned for disobeying the rule he made Aunt Eva sew the wretched badge on our coats.

I hated wearing the star and got quite worked up about it. Nobody needed to explain any more what living in freedom meant. On the sidewalks it was just awful how German soldiers would berate and ridicule any citizen with a yellow star. Soldiers would brush so closely to these unfortunates they were pushed into the gutter. Next we found ourselves unable to use parks, pools, cinemas, theatres, museums and libraries. There wasn't much normal life left.

It wasn't long before we were forbidden to ride on public transport. Our homes were no longer places of sanctuary or solace, just places to worry what more could be done to us.

Families would be called out of their houses by drum rolls to listen to some new proclamation. We continually wondered what would come next. One day it was announced all Jews had to hand in their jewellery, silverware and other valuables. There was a roaring outcry against this, but we knew the demand would be enforced to the last teapot. Some people held out a hope that paintings and furniture were not included in this edict. "They were not mentioned. Do you think the Germans will take these too?" they asked.

I was now eleven and did not fully grasp what all this meant, but a childish concept of evil overtook me.

The German bureaucrats were making headway delving into the records of Jewish citizenry, and suddenly my father's business loomed large on the screen. The Germans began to organize the takeover of Jewish undertakings and appointing Dutch Nazis to run them. Nothing was missed; factories, warehouses, stores, bank accounts, property, financial assets and art were now under German control. Billions of dollars were confiscated, destined for the German war machine.

What a brilliant and simple move on the part of the Germans; they acquired assets almost effortlessly by spreading anti-Semitism throughout the occupied countries of Europe. All the madness and cruelty were merely cunning subterfuges for the enrichment of Hitler's war chest.

The legality of stripping citizens of their rightful possessions did not enter the enemy's head, nor was any attempt made to compensate the owners, most of whom were left helpless and penniless. Many gas faucets were turned on by those unable to tolerate the terror and loss.

One of the biggest shocks to the Dutch population was that some of their closest neighbours were embracing German ideals and giving support to the Nazis. This hit people in the pit of their stomachs and, along with the often savage behaviour of the Germans, destroyed the hope and spirit of many Dutch people. However, I have to proclaim loudly that the majority of Hollanders stoutly resisted the Germans.

The van Zuiden family had lived a secular life, even though Mother had her religious moments. One could not deny our early forebears were of a more orthodox bent. Father, with his usual clear thinking, did not deceive himself and reasoned, "Before long we will be recognized as Jews and we will be targeted." He was so right.

He had been expecting an order to hand over the business, and without any prior notice a Dutch Nazi arrived one morning in 1941 and announced he was the new manager. It was a grotesque scene. The new man was disabled and could hardly get around; he had not one ounce of department store management experience. The only bright spot in the shattering day was that my family was allowed to stay in the living accommodation above the store.

I was still in Amersfoort, but I knew what was happening. Father had to look on with anguish as the new manager raped the bank accounts and day by day ran the store into the ground.

Father refused to take this move lying down. His organizational talents jumped into play the minute the Dutch Nazi took over the store. He discussed with friends and trusted managers a grand plan, and without hesitation all agreed. These good souls were willing to hide our household furnishing and possessions, and farmer friends agreed to keep The Sun's business inventory in their barns. Secrecy was paramount and the plan was hatched. Father arranged for a huge barge to be moored on the canal in front of the store. In the dead of night, he and his managers, Scholten and Smit, stealthily loaded part of the inventory and personal goods onto the barge. The boat quietly floated down the canal to the waiting barns in the countryside many kilometres away. We all thought of this evacuation as a test of faith, and Father announced, "It's in the lap of the gods whether we ever see these goods again."

Our Nazi manager was so inexperienced, or perhaps too busy looting the bank accounts, he gave no sign of noticing that part of the inventory was no longer on the shelves.

The neighbours thought Marius van Zuiden was sitting at home licking his wounds and watching all the bad moves the new manager made. In fact, employees had introduced him to the local Resistance units and Father helped them with small tasks. It quickly became clear that the riskiest part of volunteering was knowing who could be trusted. Already an atmosphere of doubt pervaded our once-sleepy town. Someone in fact did report Father to the authorities and he was no longer able to help because he was being watched. He felt even more his days of freedom were numbered.

I visited home regularly while I was still allowed to travel by train, but was still living full time in Amersfoort. Pretty soon the de Vrieses were registered as a Jewish family, and that included me. Before I knew what hit me I was thrown out of my wonderfully progressive school. Schools had slipped under German authority and the headmaster was forced to announce, "Jewish children are poisoning our learning atmosphere and can no longer attend school." I didn't know how I was poisoning the air, but I did know it was my last day at school. Some Jewish teachers bravely set up studies for the expelled pupils, but the daily harassment directed at the teachers soon made the temporary classrooms untenable. And so I never finished Grade 5.

Jews had already lost their cars, but now a new edict forced any citizen with an automobile to give it up on demand. I had been roller skating and walking to school because Uncle Willem feared the next edict would be to turn in bicycles. My bike was sitting nicely hidden behind a stack of canvases at a local artist's studio.

I hung around bored and morose, grieving for the schooling so violently plucked from me. There was no one to play with and I couldn't concentrate or read.

Many Dutch people, such as our artist friend who had hidden my bike, extended personal kindnesses. Out of necessity, active resistance intensified as the occupation proceeded. It was all kept highly secret but somehow we knew what was going on. As Father had found out, the biggest problem thwarting these activities was not knowing which citizens had Nazi sympathies. Or in other words, who could be trusted. Almost immediately it became clear that those who were caught helping Jews were shown no mercy. They were imprisoned or shot on the spot, and often their homes were burned so that the rest of their family suffered. To help anyone brought on terrible risk, and yet these citizen heroes did not flinch when help was needed. The imposition of terror and cruelty were now tools of war.

Commentary

The same cattle cars I saw in Amersfoort were to see more horrifying duty when they later transported about 117,000 Dutch Jews and other victims to places with exotic names such as Auschwitz, Sobibor, Bergen Belsen, Buchenwald, and Ravensbruck. There was also a camp called Neuengamme to which political prisoners were sent. The mass killing machines were not up and running yet and the camp occupants in the meantime were subjected to forced labour, starvation, or vicious beatings. Much of this ill treatment ended in death anyway. It was not until the 1942 Wannsee Conference that Adolph Eichmann was delegated to officially organize the mechanized mass killing of Jews, Gypsies, homosexuals and other opponents, such as Jehovah Witnesses. I knew none of these things as I stood that day watching the pitiful Russian and Ukrainian prisoners.

It was a miracle when after the war our possessions, down to precious photo albums, paintings and just plain money were all returned to Father intact. There was only one spoiler; Dad's long-time barber refused to return a virtually new radio/record player, claiming that Father had given it to him. He viciously added that the Jews had learned nothing.

Sientje just before leaving for Overveen

Marius and Sientje van Zuiden as a young couple

Henny and Meta (left) with neighbours, a year before going underground

Marius before going into hiding

Henny's fiance, Herman Parigger

Dr. and Mrs. Mettrop after the war

Karel (Carl) Keuning

Uncle Carl's magnificent 1939 Packard

CHAPTER 4

BEATING THEM TO IT

Father came to see me in Amersfoort, travelling on the still-operating trains. He told me he came because he missed me, but by listening through doors or hiding in closets I discovered his visit had another purpose. He wanted to impress on Uncle and Aunt that all of us should go into hiding. He told Uncle Willem, "We should not be sitting ducks for whatever is to come." It was not difficult to see the Germans had no good intentions for any Dutch people, not only the Jews. It was far too late now for our families to immigrate to America.

Rumours were trickling in about concentration camps that were being set up throughout Europe, and although we did not seriously believe death was in store for the inmates, we could not ignore the reports of executions.

The stark reality of our situation pounded on my father's brain and was no longer denied by his brothers and sister. With such tragic daily evidence before our eyes, Father roared, "Anyone who is optimistic is either a fool or naïve and misplacing his reason!" He kept hammering his thoughts home and I repeatedly asked him to explain his worries so that I could understand them.

Our Amsterdam relatives told Father they saw some of their neighbours being taken away by German authorities. Each person was allowed a small case and, astonishingly, any musical instrument they owned. These raids, which always took place at night, were carried out by the Gestapo and the Dutch police. Most of the policemen had to be forced to take part in this violence, but the Nazi sympathisers among them did so willingly.

These performances were accompanied by shouting, screams, and the thud of truncheons. People not obeying fast enough were shot without a moment's hesitation. Yelping police dogs on the scene paralyzed these poor souls from any thought of resistance. Each detainee was pushed into a police van. Uncle Sam told Father normal law and order had broken down in Amsterdam and no one was protesting or trying to stop the seizures. If you were Jewish, you were taken. The nets drew in everyone, including the sick, the elderly and the children.

The Jewish population was next subjected to a six p.m. curfew, and Father told me this was to make families easier targets for the night time round ups. These raids became known as *razzias*, and seemingly could not stand the light of day. They began in the ethnic areas of Amsterdam and before long had spread across Holland. The fear of a possible raid increased day by day. Jewish families knew and dreaded that the pounding at the front door could come at any time. The neighbours would hear the Germans screaming, "Open the door you damn Jews." The orders, given in Dutch and German, echoed throughout the night.

Each time I saw my father he was more tense. The whole family was worried about him. One Saturday, he arrived and told us in a serious voice, "The time has come for counter action." There was no opposition from any quarter. He gave Uncle a Resistance contact name and told him in a breaking voice, "You must immediately look for places to hide, and make arrangements for Fred and the girls to disappear."

Father had been in touch with all members of our extended family, demanding they too make arrangements to go into hiding. Some refused, some took too long to react, and some said they did not wish to endanger the lives of fellow Dutch by hiding with them.

The political climate was changing because more Dutch were sympathizing with the Germans. The increase in Fascism seemed to bear a direct relationship to German success on the battlefields, in the air, and on the high seas. Dutch turncoats made it their business to report Jewish families, whether neighbours or not, and this made the *razzias* more frequent and efficient.

It was around this period that Father finalized his plans to go into hiding with Arjay. Little sister Annemie was to go alone to a couple who had kids of their own. I was to go alone, too, and leave from Uncle's home.

The words "going into hiding" entered my life; they meant disappearing off the face of the earth.

The first to leave were my cousins Henny and Meta. The date of their departure into the great unknown — July 13th, 1942 — will stay with me forever. It was my family's first grand step to stay out of the Nazi's destructive hands. The girls, minus their yellow stars, ignored the curfew and walked down our street accompanied by Henny's fiancé, Herman. To me it seemed as though they disappeared into the ether. I was repeatedly warned not to ask any questions. The rule was that none of us was to contact any of the others once we went into hiding. Father and Uncle Willem drummed the chilling truth into us by saying over and over again, "When you have no knowledge, you lessen the risk. Under torture, you can't reveal what you don't know."

Exactly one week after Meta and Henny left, I was told that I would be next. Herman came for me at six p.m., and I, too, disappeared. Aunt Eva had torn the hated star off my raincoat, given me a supply of harsh soap and clothing, and admonished me, "Stay out of the Nazi's hands."

Patting my head, Uncle Willem whispered, "Be brave Fred, Aunt and I will leave in a week."

There was a huge *razzia* in Amersfoort five days after the de Vrieses left. It made me sick to think we had played it almost too close.

Before I disappeared Uncle Willem had recovered my bike from its hiding place. Herman and I cycled to the van der Pol home on the outskirts of Amersfoort. I knew this couple because Uncle and Aunt had shopped at their dairy farm for many years and thought of them as good friends.

Herman told me I must fully trust the van der Pols and patiently explained they would give us instructions about my first hiding address. Right then and there it came home to me that the Resistance was well established in Holland.

Aart and Janise van der Pol welcomed us naturally, just as if we had stopped by for coffee. They too had been primed to ask few questions. I stuffed down the offered cookies and milk and listened intently as they told Herman where to take me. This was my first step on the underground highway. At the time, I had not the slightest concept I would be on this road for 791 days and 15 hours.

Mrs. van der Pol was my first encounter with a surrogate mom, and I needed no coaching to accept her as a kindly aunt or mother figure. I sensed too that the van der Pols hadn't given a second thought to the risks of harbouring me. We had no chance to talk, but I am sure they saw it as their duty to help anyone oppressed or persecuted.

Herman was another righteous person. I never heard him gripe or question his duty to help the de Vries family. He would have helped even if he had not been engaged to Henny. He was raised a Protestant in what was then Czechoslovakia. He was working on a doctorate in classical languages but moved to Holland when he saw the Germans encouraging anti-Semitism in the Sudetenland area where he lived. Herman resumed his studies at Utrecht University, where he met and fell in love with Henny. He spoke perfect Dutch and the two announced their intention to marry once the war and Nazism were over.

Some Jewish people in Germany and Holland were trying to escape ethnic classification by marrying non-Jews, but it didn't work. Perhaps one might get away with it based on a one-eighth blood tie, but nothing more. Father had checked our history and found his great grandfather was identified as Jewish, so there was no escape for me under the Nuremberg edicts.

We left the van der Pol farm after an hour or so with a new destination. I didn't let on to Herman that I was actually excited about getting out of my daily tutoring at home. We two chatted away as we cycled some fifteen kilometres. Herman could see I was deluding myself about the seriousness of the situation. He shocked me out of my dream world when he said gently, "It was planned to hide you at the family farm of two of your teachers, but at the last minute they refused to take you." This rejection scared me, but I could not blame my teachers for losing their nerve. I sobered up quickly; going into hiding was not just a break from lessons.

Herman was doing his best to keep my spirits up by preparing me for any events that might come. Just the same, within a few hours I was feeling like a criminal. I was sure everybody who passed us knew exactly what we were up to. I dreaded running into someone we knew and I became more edgy with each kilometre. "The smallest bad luck and our game will be up," I whispered to myself.

I must have been thinking out loud because Herman suddenly leaned over and said, "Don't be miserable, you were doing the right thing pretending to be on an adventure. Being scared is silly and only for young kids." His message sunk in and I began play-acting with a bravado I never knew I had. I was going to be all right!

Herman chose this moment to tell me in his school masterly voice that I could no longer use the surname van Zuiden. "It's all right to use Fred," he said, "but you'll have to take the name of the family hiding you, or whatever name they give you." He saw my surprised look and said simply, "It will be safer for everyone that way."

We arrived at Terschuur village and I was quietly handed over to a wholesale grain merchant family. I could show no emotion about Herman abandoning me; I had blank, cold feelings about what the next stage of my life would bring. I managed an indifferent thank you to him for bringing me and we gave each other a firm handshake. I turned to the couple welcoming me, giving them my full attention. I only vaguely wondered when I would see Herman again.

The van der Borns were good, solid, working people with a fine reputation in the grain business. They were kindly and immediately set about making me feel at home, even though I was to be with them for only a few days. Just the same, Mr. van der Born believed we should go over some safety precautions and showed me a closet I was to climb into if a stranger came to the house. They forbade me to play outside or go near the granary, where they dealt with their customers.

What struck me most was that the family's conversation was generously sprinkled with references to the Lord. This was new behaviour to me and I did my best not to let them see I found this out of the ordinary. I was well and truly in the bosom of a religious family, and not just the Sunday variety.

I soon began to wonder how families willing to take in strangers were recruited. Besides the risks, none of them would even know how long they would have to hide these strangers. If there were children in the household, how would the parents explain away the visitors or control their tongues? I imagined a stranger coming into my family home and knew it would disrupt our life.

During this time, I gained a huge respect for religion. I supposed people willing to give sanctuary were mainly recruited through their churches. I wondered if such people were given the choice of who they took in. The Germans were also persecuting thousands of non-Jewish Dutch citizens; homosexuals, gypsies, and Seventh Day Adventists, so many of them went into hiding too. Other groups seeking sanctuary were able bodied men trying to avoid the Nazi's forced labour factories, artists, writers, musicians, doctors, and various professionals who refused to swear allegiance to the Nazis.

The van der Born's son, Wim, told me that sometimes it was impossible to find stable hiding places for long periods, and short-term sanctuaries were continually in demand. There could be no thought of posting advertisements for hiding places. Wim confided he was deeply involved with the Resistance movement, and I sensed this underground group was already well organized and efficient. Now that I knew Wim was a Resistance man, I was scared I might reveal his name if I was under torture.

My new van der Born family, like so many Dutch, lived over their business. I felt very comfortable with the family and tried to fit in by helping my kindly mom, Mrs. van der Born, with her chores. Wim, however, was worried that sooner or later some of the customers would notice me around the premises. It just wasn't possible for me to hide all day long.

Even so I was surprised when after a few days Wim told me he had reported to the Resistance that the granary was not secure enough. It was not long before another short-term house was arranged for me. I was warned I would probably be moved several times over the next few months.

The pace of my life quickened. I would have preferred to stay in the bosom of one family for a long period, but I saw some threat would always come along and I would be off again. I don't think I could have become any closer to the van der Borns in these few days, so it was hard to leave. Saying goodbye was already becoming a part of me.

Wim was as good as his word. He put my bike in the trunk of his huge 1939 Chevrolet and off we went. My thrill at riding in his splendid car softened the blow of the departure.

I was astonished when we arrived at the tiny Gelderland farmhouse that was to be my next home; I could swear our Chevy was larger. I had never seen such a small house, but then I was getting used to all kinds of new things in my life. Forbearance had entered my being, and I wished that my father could be here to see me maturing.

My new home was also in the Terschuur area, not far from the van der Born's. This house held only the bare necessities of life. I immediately worried how I was going to fit into this miniscule household, especially as I would have to stay inside most of the time. But then I noticed the vegetable garden, and I no longer felt so uneasy when I thought of the good food this family would no doubt serve.

Wim told me the owners, named Janssen, were a poor young couple but with hearts of gold, and warned me that I would find them very religious. Indeed, when we ate, Our Father was spoken with deep, ringing sincerity, both at the beginning and end of the meal. The Janssens were simple souls. They kept their little house very clean, made their own bread and feasted on the fresh vegetables. Perhaps I am the only person in the world who noticed they cleaned the floor with the same cloth that cleaned everything else in their cramped home. But none of us cared about these things any more.

It was good for me to learn what poverty was really about. My eyes were opened to many tenets of a simple life. I discovered that water did not always come from a tap; here it flowed from the outdoor pump and the rain barrel. I also found out that lavatory paper was a luxury; the outhouse was supplied with a stack of cut newspapers. Each night I slept directly on the kitchen floor covered with a blanket. I never complained to Wim about this, but he could see how Spartan life was and decided to look for another place for me. Despite their meagre means, nothing could take away the goodness of this couple who so willingly sheltered me.

I became fond of my sweet new mom and was not altogether happy when Wim arrived in my favourite auto to move me after only two weeks. The Janssens gave me clean clothing and helped pack my bike in the trunk. I bid the family an emotional farewell hugging them tightly; I never saw those kind people again.

Once on our way, Wim told me we were going to the local village doctor. "They will pretend they have adopted you because you lost your parents in the Rotterdam bombing," he explained. My heart jumped for joy when I quickly realized this meant I could play outside and return to being a normal child, running around like all the other kids. I was excited.

Pretty soon we were outside an impressive 1910 style gentleman's residence in Voorthuizen. Once again we had not driven far, perhaps five kilometres, and we were still in Gelderland Province. A tall, good looking, black-haired woman opened the door, welcoming me with open arms and a big hug. In a lovely warm voice she said, "Just call me Mom." All her movements were dramatic, and I fell in love with her from the start.

Of course I gained a new dad too, Dr. Mettrop, who was always busy and harried. He generally had no time to sit down even at mealtimes. It was totally left to Moms, as I called her, to take care of me along with her very cute seven-year-old daughter, Yosha. The two ladies devoted much time and love to me and I settled comfortably into all their routines. I secretly thought sweet Yosha was a bit spoiled, but perhaps I was a little jealous of her. In any event, we two played happily together for hours, hardly wanting to go in to eat. I fantasized I was playing with my own sister and I fleetingly wondered if sweet little Annemie was happy with her underground family.

I had been in hiding for three weeks. So far my sanctuaries had been in the Province of Gelderland, and I came to love the lush green countryside dotted with woods and charming little villages. The few adults I met were cheerful and often stopped to have a few words with me. In Voorthuizen, the local children were always willing to play, and I think they were happy to have someone new in their ranks.

The Mettrops did not send me to school, using the excuse that I was still distraught over losing my parents in the bombing raids. However, they gave me an education of a different kind — one that would not have fit into a school curriculum. In an academic and professional way, both Dr. and Mrs. Mettrop took turns in teaching me to lie. Soon I could spout any plausible story that came to mind without blushing or hesitating. I practised making every contact believe me without a flick of an eye.

I absorbed this behaviour modification like a sponge. I knew my survival might depend on being able to think on my feet. I could see this facility to lie might also work the other way, and I giggled as I imagined myself being able to recognize a con man in two seconds flat. Here I was, eleven years old, honing my skills to deceive. And all the while playing with the local children and going shopping with Moms.

The next three months flew by in the company of the delightful, free-thinking Mettrops. Such people were new in my experience and I was exhilarated. I knew I would never forget this couple or this place.

I am probably being unfair to single out the Mettrops for such high praise when all my protectors had risked their lives and possessions. But this family imbued in my bones the importance of a life in freedom, however modest. I learned the thrill of having outrageous ideas and freely expressing them. They made me understand that my present life, living like a hunted animal, was merely a diversion to be endured. I was only twenty kilometres from the de Vries home in Amersfoort, but with my new confidence I knew I could cope with the continual worry of being recognized.

Another highlight of my stay was playing with the neighbours' children. The treat of having dinner at their homes sometimes was almost too much excitement to bear. When eating with the grocer's children I answered all kinds of questions about the way my parents died in Rotterdam's ruthless bombing. I told childish white lies as I came up with thrilling versions of the devastating bombardment. I indeed became skilful at my new talent and made full use of my coaching. But one day I slipped up and the grocer caught me out on some simple fact. Thankfully his wife figured I was just confused and told her husband not to push me. I began looking forward to the time when I didn't have to be afraid of telling the unadorned truth.

Moms generally produced three meals a day and I hung around her skirts trying to help. Once again I was acquiring a new talent; I had never tried cooking, nor had it even entered my head. Cooking meant shopping, so off we went. I learned how to pick out vegetables and meat, especially oxtails, which the whole family were crazy about. By the autumn of 1942 food was noticeably less plentiful. Through our Resistance contact, I was able to arrange for Moms to visit my old Amersfoort neighbours who were hiding tinned goods for Uncle and Aunt de Vries. Moms made her visit under a cloud of secrecy and she assured me her foray would give no clue to my whereabouts. I think she really enjoyed her cloak and dagger mission, and Dr. Mettrop teased her that evening.

Medical personnel were given a small gas allowance for patient visiting, and I bugged the doctor to take me on his daily trips. He made me wait outside but I didn't care; it was such a pleasure to get out into the beautiful local scenery, which was very different from my home area in Northern Holland.

On one occasion, Dr. Mettrop was called to tend a British fighter pilot who had bailed out too late for his parachute to fully deploy. I went along, but by the time we reached the poor man he was dead. The good doctor took the pilot's signet ring and flying boots explaining he would try to find the parents at war's end. I was quick to pick up on his chivalry and I realized it was another of Dr. Mettrop's life-enhancing lessons.

This idyllic period was not to last. It came to a shattering end in early November while Moms and I were on an egg-buying mission at a country farm. There was suddenly a crash of metal colliding with metal and we all looked round in time to see a pick-up truck sideswipe a tractor as it skidded into the farmyard. The driver and his passenger looked around and seemed to be gesturing at me. But they turned round quickly and left, probably realizing they were on the wrong road.

Moms told me later that the driver had shouted out of the cab, "That boy could be Jewish too!" She loudly protested to the other customers that the man was yelling stupid things about her adopted son. She was on her guard though. We paid for the eggs, left the farm casually, and tried to appear calm while cycling home.

Like lightning life changed. The Mettrops insisted that Wim van der Born move me immediately from the imminent danger.

Commentary

THE RESISTANCE: While in hiding, I came to realize many others were being hidden in the area around Amersfoort. I later learned people were being concealed all over Holland and in Belgium. Not one of us ever spoke about whom we suspected of being a Resistance person, or what families seemed to have secret guests. The folks in hiding were referred to as "undergrounders." Most of them were Jews and other persecuted minorities, but in time shot-down Allied airmen were also hidden within the Dutch population.

After the war, Father rehired all his faithful pre-war managers and engaged as many Resistance people as possible. Dad was to find many of these heroes had trouble adjusting to civilian life after the initial high of the liberation. The mundane roles of peace-time just did not suit them.

I cajoled many of these former Resistance workers to tell me about their war experiences and I was enthralled with their tales of risk and daring. One of the staff members, Tjark, told me it had been a high priority for their group to raid political prisons in order to liberate comrades who might talk under abusive interrogations. Another priority was to destroy population records at the municipal offices; the Germans manipulated such information at a whim to arrest or harass victims. Another role of the Resistance was executing Dutch collaborators. Rough justice lived all around us in those war years.

Tjark said the Germans regularly performed senselessly cruel acts in an effort to break the strong will of the Dutch Resistance. One such event took place at the Vught Concentration camp, which housed other persecuted minorities, as well as Jews. Apparently a woman had displeased some guards and was thrust into an underground bunker. In sympathy seventy-four women rushed in to join her before the doors were slammed tight. Overnight, ten women suffocated in that airless chamber. News of this atrocity spread. It enraged most Dutch people and propelled many of them into supporting the Resistance network even more.

THE DUTCH NAZI PARTY: Although only five percent of the Dutch population became active members of the Dutch Nazi Party, their presence during the German occupation allowed the Nazis virtually complete control of the Netherlands. (The Communist Party dominated the Soviet Union with a similar five percent membership.)

THE METTROPS: After the war, Dr. Mettrop followed a career in the public sector. At one time he was employed by the United Nations to give aid at the Palestinian refugee camps in the Lebanon. I caught up with him and his wife forty-five years after they had hidden me, and we connected immediately. I found them still to be articulate and their personalities as liberal as ever.

CHAPTER 5

A MAN SENT FROM HEAVEN

In less than an hour I had packed my things and Wim came to get me in the Chevrolet. I sat beside him rigid and silent. I had erected a shell around me as a way to cope with my turbulent emotions.

Wim understood that the lightning departure had upset me and kept on saying, "You shouldn't be sad or angry. Survival is your goal and the only game in town. Big boys have to be tough!"

After riding in silence for some time, Wim announced cheerfully, "You are going to Wageningen to meet two men who will take over from me in finding your hiding places." By now I had the utmost confidence in Wim and didn't look forward to dealing with the new men, Karel (Carl) Keuning and Klaas van Houten. Wim added, "They have an impressive reputation in the Resistance and they specialize in finding families to hide people, especially Jewish children." As the kilometres passed, I worried I might have a shyness attack when I had to speak to them.

We parked outside van Houten's very large house. "Hold on, Fred, I'll go and get him," said Wim. He soon came back with a tall, slightly heavy man with a moustache. He was about fifty, well dressed, and handsome. He had the air of a prosperous businessman.

I had rehearsed at least twenty times, "Good afternoon, Mr. van Houten," and was caught off guard when the man proved to be Carl Keuning. We three drove off and the large man announced, "I am your Uncle Carl from now on."

I liked him immediately and sensed he was kind. He didn't expect any answers from me. I just mumbled a few nothings now and again, but I was already feeling more comfortable.

Before long we stopped at another stately home, this one facing the Wageningen Tropical Studies University. "That's my home, Fred, and you're going to stay with me for a few days. Say good bye to Wim and jump out." My new uncle took my case, grabbed my hand, and led me into the house.

Wim drove off and I waved goodbye, not dreaming that the name of the road we were on would later be changed to honour the Supreme Commander of the Canadian forces, General Foulkes, who liberated most of Holland.

As soon as I saw the wide, heavily carpeted stairway leading to the upper floor, I knew I was in a grand residence. Two plainly dressed ladies also in their fifties greeted me. I was told to call them both "aunt." Lisa was Carl's sister, and Anna was her friend. They started fussing over me straight away. "Dinner will be ready soon, Fred," said Lisa, and she took my case. It was only then I realized how hungry I was.

Before the meal Uncle Carl took me up the grand staircase and showed me my bedroom. My clothes had been unpacked already.

"I'll keep showing you around till they call us for dinner," he said. When we went to his sitting room-cum-study, I gasped at the heavily paneled walls and shelves laden to the ceiling with books. There was a fireplace, too, with a fire crackling away in the grate. He pointed out two desks, telling me I was welcome to use the smaller one whenever I stayed at his house.

I looked around absorbing the fine furnishings. Carl opened his desk, pulled out a fistful of bills and pressed them into my hand. There must have been at least twenty dollars, a fortune for me, and I quickly told him I could not accept his largesse. "You might need it in the days to come; put it in your pocket. I'll look for a wallet for you."

A bell tinkled to summon us to the dining room, which was furnished as luxuriously as everything else in the house. I stared at the sumptuous dinner on the table. We started with soup and my cousins' lessons not to slurp came back with a bang. We then dug into mountains of well-done beef surrounded by fresh vegetables. A lovely sticky tart completed the banquet. I was definitely feeling better.

I was not to escape the custom of prayers both before and after the meal in my sumptuous new surroundings. This grand household proved no different from the others in that regard, but included the bonus of daily readings from an ancient Bible. Sometimes it was the ladies reading and sometimes Uncle Carl. All recited long parables with deep passion, touching on the present conditions of a violent war, and of a persecuted boy sitting at their table.

One day while Carl was out, his sister showed me his bedroom. In the middle was a majestic bed sinking into deep, thick white carpet. Once again there were hundreds of books interspersed with huge, colourful flower paintings. They were so marvellous, they took my breath away. I knew little about paintings but I knew I liked these. The whole bedroom was suffused with sunlight streaming through the French doors, which led to a balcony. It was becoming clear to me that people from all walks of life were helping to fight the injustices of this war.

I was quite in awe of everything. Uncle Carl's charm and great sense of humour ran through the small household. He had a way of soothing the tension, even though we could not forget for one minute the Gestapo could hammer on our door at any time. I did not really believe this grand man would keep his word about buying me a wallet. But, a few days later, he came home with a thin, black billfold smelling of fine leather.

Suddenly I was a man of means and wanted to go out and buy presents for everyone in the household. Uncle Carl said that it was not safe for me to leave the house or even to be seen at the windows. He then took me into his study for a serious talk.

"I want you to be ultra careful and keep away from the windows. This house is under constant Gestapo surveillance because Uncle Klaas and I are suspected of being part of the Dutch Resistance. Gestapo agents have already been here twice but I hid. Luckily, one of the agents noticed I was reading Hitler's book *Mein Kampf,* which put me in a better light in their eyes. Also, Klaas and I have been taken to headquarters for interrogation. Luckily, we were not separated so we didn't have to worry about keeping our stories straight. The agent said he had a huge file on our activities and that we were suspected of being enemies of the State!"

My uncles were not the type of men to be intimidated. They reacted angrily and told the interrogator that his information was false. "One way or another we bluffed our way out of the interrogation and were allowed to go home. But, we realized we would have to be ultra careful with future activities."

It was the university hothouses across the road that had lured me to the windows. I was miserable that the simple act of looking outside was denied me. The Gestapo and their collaborators had a thousand eyes aching to detect someone.

Even though I stayed at Wageningen for only five days, somehow Uncle Carl and I struck up a good friendship and he opened up new horizons to me. He would teach me about the universe and the solar systems whenever he had a spare moment. The aunts explained Carl had been a boarding school teacher, certified in at least twelve subjects. The gods had thrown me into the lap of another person destined to fill the void of my lack of schooling.

Carl and Klaas were not only Resistance partners but colleagues in a huge printing firm in Wageningen. They specialized in Christian educational works and Bibles. They had traveled together in their youth, visiting exotic places such as the Arctic regions of Northern Scandinavia and the Balkans.

Their huge printing plant had been bombed in 1940 and there was nothing left of the plant at the end of the assault. The Germans, needing to print their own propaganda, did not thwart the rebuilding of the plant.

Before I left Uncle Carl's he gave me a beautiful black leather-bound Bible that his company had printed. Carl emphasized he was not trying to convert me to Christianity; he just wanted to widen my knowledge of the Christian religion. It was also his idea that it would help me understand the devout people who would hide me. He explained that when he and Klaas arranged hiding places, they always made it clear to the kind families they had no right to indoctrinate me into a religion different from that of my parents.

Uncle said this issue was a larger problem than one might have imagined. Most of these protectors were truly religious and in their zeal could hardly control themselves from telling about their saviour.

And so, sadly, my delicious five-day sojourn with Uncle Carl and the genteel Aunts came to an end. I kept waving to the ladies long after Uncle and I had driven away. I was taken by surprise when he told me my new hiding place would be Elisabeth Homestead, a home for the mentally disabled, deeply hidden in the countryside of Lunteren.

The Homestead was a charming three-storied villa with green and white shutters and a thatched roof. It was surrounded by orchards and high pines. These trees gave me a sense of security, but in truth they offered none. The front door opened as we approached.

Commentary

After the war Carl and Klaas were decorated for saving 176 youngsters and for their incredible intelligence work. Nobody realized one of the phones in Klaas' office had a direct connection to General Eisenhower's secret Paris headquarters. Klaas was able to feed strategic information to Paris, most of it obtained by a team of female couriers innocently pedalling all over Holland.

CHAPTER 6

A DIFFERENT KIND OF ASYLUM

Elisabeth Homestead was founded by the Boelen family as a home for their mentally handicapped baby, Elisabeth. They built the villa, employed nurses to look after Elisabeth, and instructed them to take in other mental patients in order to offset expenses.

The two van Katwijk sisters ran the place, and I soon learned to trust them as my new moms, even though I addressed them both as "Aunt." Aunt Nel was a tall, buxom, handsome woman with intelligent blue eyes. Her private bed-sitting room was filled with paintings, small sculptures and fine art books. Although aloof, Nel was proud of her art knowledge and boasted about her visits to Florence.

Aunt Johanna was second in command to her sister. She was a more motherly woman but in no way lacked in charm or the gift of the gab. She left all the administrative duties to Nel but both ladies worked with the patients. I liked dogs and was thrilled when I found Johanna owned an adorable Cocker Spaniel named Rudy. I continually competed with the dog for Johanna's affection.

Once again I acquired another persona. I now became Pieter van Katwijk, their nephew from the university city of Leiden. I immediately became very comfortable with my new name and thought it suited me better than Fred van Zuiden. Straight away I grasped I had moved into another religious household. There were prayers at both ends of the three daily meals, along with weekly church visits. The sisters did not have an easy time with their mentally disturbed patients, but the ladies kept calm and there was always a disciplined but cheery mood at Elisabeth Homestead.

I spent most of my days mingling with the patients and found one not more intriguing or bizarre than the next. Diet was the adult daughter of a well-known chocolate manufacturer. She was very bright on the one hand, but troubled by music ringing in her ears, classical at that. Diet was determined she was going to teach me French, and I did get a little way with the language from this ambitious lady. I practised my French on the patients but never got any response from them.

Another woman in particular captured my interest, and I often sat by sixty-year-old Mrs. Nutby, who suffered from delusions of grandeur. Her father was English and she continually regaled me with tales of high society, probably most of them imaginary.

Our star patient was the villa's namesake, twenty-seven-year-old Elisabeth, who referred to herself as Liesje. Her facial expression immediately revealed her severe mental handicap. I had to get used to looking at her and at the same time ignoring her disability. She sat rocking her body to and fro, and had the habit at any time, day or night, of calling for her tea. "Liesje wants tea. LIESJE WANTS TEA! **LIESJE WANTS TEA!**" she repeated in an increasingly louder pitch. She would go on, and on, and on. At night time, she would accompany her shouts with much shaking and rattling of her locked bedroom door. Aunt Johanna would finally arrive with the tea and calm her down. I slept in the attic directly above Liesje, so was continually woken by this commotion.

Her eating habits both fascinated and repulsed me. She would uncontrollably stuff food in her mouth. She never chewed anything and invariably choked several times at each meal trying to swallow and gasp for air at the same time. It was a continual battle for Nel to hold Liesje's head steady and remove food from her mouth at the same time.

Then there was Liesje's persistent belching and farting. Not even the long-suffering Aunt Nel could control that, so we all learned to get used to it. She caused uproars by spontaneously undressing or leaving her panties down after visiting the toilet. She was immensely strong and it was difficult for her nurses to restrain or dress her.

Despite her peculiarities and antics, I counted Liesje as a friend and felt she was happy in her own world. Aunt Johanna explained to me insane people often lived to a ripe old age because they don't have to cope with the worries of real life. Her parents never came to visit. We were all thankful because we suspected they favoured the wrong side in this war.

The Homestead was also harbouring a Jewish couple from The Hague. Lex and Rita, who were in their mid forties, occupied a bed-sitting room on the mezzanine floor. They were a sad couple with not much hope left in their bones. They kept to themselves, even doing their own cooking. The savoury smells drove me wild and I continually lived in hope of some scraps coming my way. None were ever offered. Lex sometimes gave me school work but he was generally in a foul mood and I shied away.

It was dawning on me that the Homestead meal offerings were pretty sparse. I became hungrier as the days passed.

Aunt Nel probably wasn't meant to tell me, but she found out my cousins Meta and Henny were in hiding at Meu-Lunteren only ten kilometres away. Knowing they were close buoyed me, even though it was out of the question to visit them. Uncle Carl heard the news, too, and arranged for the girls to send me lessons. Aunt Nel dutifully cycled the lesson materials back and forth, and I found myself enjoying learning again.

Matters were not going so well for Lex and Rita. One day they mysteriously moved out of the Homestead to a room in the village. It was their bad luck to be seen by a collaborator they had known years earlier in The Hague. No time was wasted in reporting them. Both Lex and Rita tried to commit suicide, but they did not succeed. They were arrested, and I presumed they were taken to a camp. They were an unhappy couple to start with and I couldn't imagine how they would find the strength to cope with their imprisonment. I never did learn their fate.

Day-to-day activities at the villa sometimes produced exciting moments, such as when a baby arrived out of the blue — literally and metaphorically. The little one had been found freezing on a wet doorstep in Amsterdam. A note said the parents were scheduled for a death camp transport and they pleaded for someone to take care of the three-day-old girl. No names were given for child or parents, which added to the mystery.

The poor little thing had bronchitis and was blue from the cold, but by whatever baffling manner, she found her way to our haven in the woods. We all fell in love with the helpless little soul. Nel and Johanna rounded up clothing, bedding and a splendid baby carriage from neighbours who asked no questions. Without any fuss we agreed the baby looked like a Betty, and that's what we called her. There wasn't one of us, sane or otherwise, who did not take part in nurturing her back to health. Daily, she would be bundled up and tucked into the baby carriage. It was usually my task to push her pram around outside in the fresh air. Betty recovered splendidly. I wondered what course her life would take. I knew she was too young to remember her Elisabeth Homestead family, or the skinny boy who wheeled her around the grounds under a pale wintry sun.

On my twelfth birthday in November 1942, there was another exciting event. In my highly secret life I had a visitor. Dr. Mettrop, on his rounds, had brought Moms to Elisabeth Homestead to help celebrate the day. She arrived with a huge quantity of food, clothing and puzzles and I could not stop jumping all over her trying to thank her for the wonderful surprise. "How did you know where I was?" I cried. The most she would say was, "The Resistance moves in mysterious ways."

The day was full of hugs and kisses and my childish joy was total when Uncle Carl arrived on the scene. I had heard no knock. He, too, came laden with gifts. I immediately tried on the heavy woollen overcoat he handed me and twirled around the room showing it off. He had brought winter shoes, too, in just the right size. I could not bear to take off my new coat and shoes and kept them on until I went to bed that night.

The day of warmth and excitement nourished my spirit and strengthened my will to keep going. Nobody had realized yet that I was almost continually hungry. I kept quiet about it because Uncle had told me not to complain. There was food at Elisabeth Homestead, but not enough to satisfy a growing boy.

I made friends with Jan, a neighbour's boy. Having a friend near my own age made me feel like a kid again. Because most of my time was spent with adults, I didn't always know how to see things in a childish light. I had missed not being able to share youthful secrets or just plain horse around with other boys.

Jan Koerts lived at the edge of the woods surrounding Elisabeth Homestead. Sadly, his two brothers had been killed in a glider collision high over Central Java, where his parents had been on a tour of duty in the then-Dutch East Indies.

Jan and I played with the lead soldiers and miniature aluminum planes that Carl had given me. We invented fierce war games acted out in shallow sand ditches, fortifications and rail lines. Jan ran the power from his family's cottage and together we built our battle sites. We used large pebbles to bomb the war zones, and if we had too many casualties we simply made more soldiers. I accomplished this by melting abandoned lead pipes and pouring the liquid lead into moulds Uncle Carl had given me. Occasionally the Koerts family had me to dinner and I wondered if his parents noticed how I gulped down the food.

Jan was a bright fellow and we shared each other's boyish fantasies, but I was always under the strain of not revealing who I was. Uncle Carl had really ground into me I must never deviate from my cover story. Jan's big dream was to own a racing car, and he would bug me with a thousand technical details about the MG, which was his favourite.

The food supply worsened in Holland and trickled down to the Homestead. Nowadays I always went to bed hungry. My little cot was under the thatched roof where they stored the winter apples. I would pick my way through the scattered fruit, careful not to bruise it. If I had not had apples to munch on, my health would have suffered further.

When Lex and Rita were still with us I frequently went to their room, not only drawn by food smells but to listen to BBC broadcasts on their illegal miniature radio. We were desperate for news on how the war was proceeding. At night we heard all kinds of planes flying overhead, along with violent machine gunning. We thought the planes must be Luftwaffe night fighters attacking RAF bombers as they made their way each night to bomb Germany.

One time we heard a bigger than usual commotion and more machine guns than ever. Bright flashes reflected through the windows. Just after midnight there was loud banging on the front door and the bell rang continuously; such a disturbance did not augur well at this time of night. We peered over the balustrade in our nightclothes, afraid we were being raided. None of us had heard vehicles approaching. I was ready to flee to my attic, kick away the entry ladder and disappear into my hiding niche. We held our breath as Aunt Nel marched staunchly downstairs and opened the front door.

There was a loud babble of German, which we all sweated through. I couldn't get out of my head that the Germans would find my warm bed and know someone was hiding close by.

The tension broke when we understood our German visitor was claiming he was a downed Messerschmitt 110 pilot. Nel could speak German and gathered this was his forty-third bail out, but this time he had landed in one of our trees. His helmet strap and parachute cords were wrapped around his neck. He said he almost strangled by the time he got his knife out of his pocket and cut through the noose. Then he had fallen heavily to the ground and was worried his leg was broken. Dazed as he was, he limped over to the lights shining from the villa. The pilot told Nel he was worried about his navigator whom he hadn't seen bail out, and that he had hit a British plane which must have crashed in our vicinity.

The minute Aunt Nel let him in he demanded to use the phone. He called his Brussels Air Base to arrange for a military pick up and sat in the hall waiting for it. I could see the pilot was relishing a few moments of respite as he chatted with Nel, telling her he had been born into a noble Munich family. With fabled German efficiency the military pick up came within ninety minutes. We remained hanging silently over the balustrade. Although none of us spoke German, we somehow got the gist of what he was saying. When he left, we all sighed with relief. Not even Liesje started her regular nightly screaming and rocking.

The Homestead activities started at dawn, so each of us was expected to go to bed early. I was never tired till later, and mostly prowled around exploring the Homestead's nooks and crannies. One night I got a whiff of cooking, which steadily grew stronger and stronger. My hungry belly had no will to resist and I descended from my attic sniffing all the way to the annex kitchen. The household used this area as a laundry and there was a huge stove to heat water. I knew all about this stove; this is where I made my replacement lead soldiers.

That night, however, there was no foundry or laundry activity, just Aunt Nel and Aunt Johanna frying a mountain of onions in a huge pan. The onions were merrily bubbling away, smelling like heaven on earth. I really startled the ladies and I don't know who was the more embarrassed or shocked, but I backed out of the door, speechless. Nothing was ever said about our dramatic encounter, and I did not get any succulent onions.

This episode brought home how hungry I really was, and I began developing childish notions of suicide. I smuggled a bread knife from the kitchen and practised plunging it into my chest. Killing oneself proved more difficult than I would have thought. As I worked myself up to the deed my will to live came back. Or perhaps it was just lack of courage.

There had been no Gestapo raids in Henny and Meta's vicinity or near the Homestead. Because of this, I begged Nel to ask Carl to allow me to walk to the girls once a week, even though it was two hours each way. Approval was granted and I was soon enjoying the sense of freedom I got from being away from the Homestead for a few hours.

The girls were not being kept short of food, so on each visit I got a nourishing lunch and several gorgeous deserts to tickle my sweet tooth. They had actually saved this food from their previous week's meals, and in my new style I gobbled everything down the minute I saw it. I realized I was eating no better than Liesje; it didn't take long for the girls to remind me of my ugly manners. The sudden intake of better food quickly upset my stomach, so after a few visits I slowed down my voracious food attacks.

Once lunch was finished the girls used the precious time to go over my lessons and teach me new things. However well they set my weekly tasks, I still managed to get into difficulty trying to tackle the lessons on my own. During one of the visits Meta and Henny poignantly apologized for not letting me play with the neighbourhood kids during their strict tutoring regimen in Amersfoort. "I know you were being harsh for my own good," I told them, and we all hugged and shed a few tears. I probably overdid my contriteness when I suggested their fine teaching made me want to be a professor one day. But in my bones I knew the discipline of learning was ingrained forever.

Our lunch visits took place in the girls' tiny bed-sitting room at the rear of a small country home owned by Chris van Schuppen and his wife, Jo. On the way I walked by the Dutch Nazi Convention Centre at Meu-Lunteren, which was like a small open-air stadium. There were thousands of seats facing a yellow brick podium, similar to the one I had seen in newsreels showing Hitler ranting away.

The van Schuppens told me literally thousands were undergoing indoctrination at the site, spurred on by Dutch fascist leaders, including Anton Mussert. As I passed by, I could hear every word of the loud hatred being spewed out against Bolshevism, Anglo Saxons, and, of course, the eternally damned and evil Jews. Sometimes there was a change of pace and the microphones blared out fascist marching songs. I found myself walking in step with the songs and was not surprised that others were incited by the rousing music.

One day I heard the audience being exhorted to join battles on the German and Russian fronts. There was already a Dutch Division and units from other occupied or sympathizing nations. I thought the Germans probably saved thousands of their own soldiers by utilizing these foreign contingents. More German efficiency!

During my stay at Elisabeth Homestead, I realized that not all Germans had backed Hitler's doctrines. One day a German conscientious objector appeared at our villa, having escaped across the confused Dutch border when the Germans invaded. Nel encouraged us to welcome this brave man and we all went out of our way to be kind to him. He did not stay long, though, and news got back that he was shot when making a run for it during a Gestapo raid.

It always surprised me that Elisabeth's parents never got a smell that their Lunteren villa was a hive of Resistance activity. Even Liesje's sister was supposed to be a strong Nazi sympathizer, but Aunt Nel did not let this affect Liesje's care.

It was reported to Uncle Carl my weekly visits to Meta and Henny were going well. He also knew by now I was not getting enough to eat, so he worked on a plan to move me. The Resistance still deemed the girls' sanctuary safe, and in June 1943 I was told I would be moved there. I immediately became delirious about this full time reunion with my cousins and the thought of fresh farm food.

No time was wasted. Aunt Johanna packed my little case and I went round kissing all the occupants farewell. I tried to express my deep thanks to Nel and Johanna, but we were all so overcome we could not speak. Tight hugs and tears replaced words. I left Elisabeth Homestead on my bike, thanking some mysterious god for the eight months of safety spent with these dear people.

Commentary

During my time at the Homestead, Aunt Johanna let me know that thousands of German Christians were in terrible concentration camps. She told me these brave souls were mainly those who opposed the Nazification of their Protestant churches. They vehemently opposed the anti-Christian ideals and racial doctrines promoted by the Nazis.

She told me about the Reverend Martin Niemoller who had risen as a leader of these opposing churchgoers. She said originally Niemoller's opinions were tainted by his professed anti-Semitism. Most observers thought he, too, was a victim of centuries of traditional Jewish hatred springing from Jesus dying on the cross. Some writers like Robert Michael preached that this ancient belief was behind most Nazi collaboration as opposed to political differences. It surprised me that Aunt Johanna knew such a lot about this subject.

Only a minute fraction of the German population was making any effort to hide and protect Jews during the brutal regime. It was hard for me to grasp the high degree of courage those few persons must have had. I am sure I could not have measured up to such bravery.

Sixty years later, I returned to that beautiful, silent, remote area and rang the doorbell at Elisabeth Homestead's front door. While waiting on the step, I felt the home's personality had not changed. A woman in her forties opened the door.

I immediately tried to put her at ease, explaining I had come to visit the house that had played such an important role in my war years. The lady told me she and her husband had only very recently acquired the Homestead, but she had already been told that the house, now a private home, had been a hotbed of underground resistance.

My hostess was able to bring me up to date on the Elisabeth Homestead nurses. I learned Johanna had been killed on her high powered Solex motorbike. I thought to myself, that lady had obviously kept her adventurous spirit right to her dramatic end. Nel had retired to the nearby home of a baroness. I embraced my hostess and left the Homestead to continue on its path in history.

By now it was dusk and I don't know how many dark lanes I went down looking for the baroness' address. I eventually stumbled on the villa. Before I had a chance to knock, a tall, austere man dressed in black appeared. He introduced himself as the baroness' *aide de camp* and a wartime intelligence officer at Arnhem.

I was invited in and presented to an elderly, but very alert and stately woman. Sadly, she told me Aunt Nel had just died. The baroness and her *aide* then launched into their hair-raising Resistance experiences. Who would ever dream of the exciting dramas that took place in the environs of this still idyllic village?

After the war, like many others, I always felt uncomfortable meeting Dutch people who had been fascists. I would make every effort to avoid such confrontations. Sometimes I would come across pilots from both sides fraternizing and swapping experiences. It took me a long time to come to grips with the fact that people who had been in life-and-death struggles during the war, could now just chat with each other.

CHAPTER 7

A NEST OF RESISTANCE

I arrived safely at Chris and Jo van Schuppen's small, cozy cottage. I was already familiar with the place and so immediately felt at home. They were hospitable, salt-of-the-earth people with goodness stamped all over their faces. I was comfortable with my new mom in record time. Predictably, they were very religious, and continually preached to me that Jesus was the great guiding hand.

The difference between the van Schuppen home and Elisabeth Homestead was like night and day. It was great to be in this new household and I became a cheerful kid again the minute I stopped being hungry. I was now in a wonderland of home-baked bread and farm-fresh butter, cheese and eggs. There was no hint of stinting on the food. The logistics of feeding so many people as well as their own family seemed to cause no problem for the van Schuppens. They outdid themselves with their daily offerings. I eagerly jumped back into lessons in Meta and Henny's sitting room.

This cottage was even deeper in the bush than Elisabeth Homestead had been and was reached via an unpaved, rutted track off the local village road. There were no other permanent residences in the area, but there was a small vacation resort and pool across the road. The resort was on a slight hill, but the bush surrounding it was so dense it was virtually hidden.

Chris and Jo owned three summer rental cabins, as well as the cottage they lived in. These small buildings stood slightly offset behind their home. In the warm months city families with loads of kids, mainly from Haarlem, spent their holidays in these cabins. The children went wild in the unrestricted countryside, spending lots of time building castles with wide moats and long tunnels in the sandy soil.

The resort owners across the road were great friends of Chris and Jo, and they generously permitted the van Schuppens and their guests to use the pool. The kids from Haarlem were not the only ones to be thrilled about a chance to swim. The invitation was extended to us underground guests, too. Jo, who I now thought of as Aunt Jo, said it was the neighbour's way of giving comfort to those they knew were being hidden next door. For security reasons we only swam in the middle of the night; you can bet your life none of us wore a swim suit.

The other undergrounders in my new-found land of milk and honey were adults. Soon after my arrival I was introduced to three Dutch army officers — (another) Wim, Jan, and Gerrit— who had refused to report to the Germans. From time to time I would see them in the house and grounds, but like me they each slept outside in the woods. It was deemed unsafe for any of us four males to sleep in the house in case we were trapped during a raid.

As nerve wracking as our situation really was we undergrounders sometimes became bored, so we willingly helped out with the chores. One job we could not neglect was the maintaining of our sleeping holes. These two-man dugouts were about sixty metres from the house, between the pines. They were deep enough to stand up in, and we used simple wooden steps to descend. I got the daily job of raking the straw so our "mattresses" were fresh. We camouflaged the holes both day and night by placing branches and young growth trees over the top. Once in our sleeping bags we couldn't complain about our beds; they were warm and comfortable.

I did my very best to keep the straw in a good state but our sleeping holes were proving not so healthy. We were all squeamish about the black beetles and awoke with body and face bites most mornings. We had an awful time wiping off the sticky stuff that oozed from their legs; it clung to our skin like glue. We might have been able to put up with this, but when water started seeping up through the ground and soaking the straw, we abandoned the dugouts. The officers had small tents, so we found a natural clearing deep in the woods and made camp.

I shared a tent with Wim. I had already heard he was daring and brave, now I found out he was very religious. He insisted we pray before bedding down, so I joined him and fervently begged the Lord's help to survive. I was so moved by the impassioned prayers welling up from unfathomable depths in Wim, tears came to my eyes. I suppose in a way, if ever I prayed this was where I learned how to do it.

The officers soon grasped I was quite knowledgeable about the war and we chatted often. After Holland capitulated in 1940 the Germans had imprisoned the Dutch military; however, they let them go after a few months because it was too costly to maintain them. Then the Germans got into their heads that any officers released might form the core of an underground military force to support the Allies when and if they invaded Europe. In any event, my officer friends said the Germans issued a proclamation in 1942 demanding that all Dutch officers report back to locations throughout Holland. The Resistance soon learned this was a trick and warned the men against reporting back. Unfortunately, many did not hear the warning and fell into the trap. About 10,000 officers, including generals, were incarcerated in camps in Stanislaw, Poland, for the remainder of the war.

Those who refused to report mingled back into the population or, as my three new buddies had done, went into hiding. My head was full of stories about the Dutch Resistance and I soon realized the van Schuppens were very involved with that group. One of the officers, Jan from Nijmegen, was a bright, pleasant guy who seemed to be pleased that I was so interested in his activities. He was an electronics expert and besides preparing explosives for the Resistance arsenal he helped the van Schuppens with their batteries and secret radios.

All of us were overjoyed to have contact with the outside world and every day we sat around one of the radios listening to the free world Radio Orange broadcasts coming out of London.

The other officer was actually the van Schuppen's son, Gerrit, hiding in his own home. His code name was *Zwarte* (Black) Gert, so that's what I called him. We all heard a thousand times how crazy he was about his very pregnant wife, Rosa. I got on well with Gert and we spent much time together working on the chores. For some reason he disliked Meta and Henny and I could never get to the bottom of it. Perhaps it was a personality issue for I knew my cousins could get pretty bossy, and I had seen Gert in a really foul mood more than once.

I often heard him in loud arguments with his gentle parents. The rest of us made allowances for Gert's disposition simply because he was also so deeply involved in his Resistance activities. Uncle Carl told me these fellows suffered significant stress because they never knew if their colleagues were secret collaborators. It sometimes got so bad that many guys refused to trust their parents, siblings, friends and colleagues. Treason came from all levels of Dutch society.

Wim, the officer I shared a tent with, seemed to be active in the Resistance at a higher level of the organization. I found him an exotic fellow, to say the least. I soon discovered he sometimes wore women's clothing and I assumed it was his cover when he went on assignments. Although I was only twelve, I had already been told about homosexuality so I was not too shocked when Gert clarified the situation. He told me Wim had had a so-called passionate affair with a German Luftwaffe officer in order to gain entry into the Soesterberg air base. The Germans had built a huge munitions depot on this airfield and stocked it with bombs intended for London and other centres in Great Britain.

Back in 1941 Wim had spearheaded the plan to demolish the Soesterberg depot. The plan succeeded brilliantly. The resulting mid-day explosion shook the ground so violently it was like an earthquake. The vibrations were felt thirty kilometres away. Wim, now known as Soesterberg Wim, kept me fascinated for days recounting the details of the planning and actual raid.

Gert told me other tales about Wim. Again dressed as a woman, he went to the famous White Restaurant in Amersfoort with his Luftwaffe lover. During dinner Wim realized the German suspected who he really was, so made a break for it. The officer gave chase and caught up to Wim as he was climbing over a fence. Although the German managed to whack his erstwhile lover on the head with his revolver, Wim escaped. But he was left with a reminder of this escapade; violent migraines plagued him ever after. I often came across him moaning from the pain and popping pills.

Life settled down in my new home and I quickly took up a routine of studying intensely the whole morning, and then escaping outside for chores. There was always a lot to do but my main duty was to chop fuel for all the stoves; and there were many! I became adept at wood chopping and acquired huge muscles from sawing large logs. Wood stacking came into play, too, and I was very proud of the artistic way I piled the logs.

As soon as families began arriving at the rental cottages, I went to find the kids, hoping some would be my age. There were usually some older children and we played together building huge sandcastles and intricate towers. No matter how much fun we were having, we stopped as soon as we heard the drone of planes and scanned the sky.

Daily, Allied planes flew high overhead leaving mysterious stratospheric contrails. We craned our necks to observe these sky-borne armadas, each of us having a dream that peace was somewhere on the horizon. Actually, our imaginations ran riot with scenes of the Allies challenging the monster force bottled up in Germany and in the helpless occupied countries. We learned from clandestine broadcasts these massive flights were bombing the hell out of enemy industrial centres. We also learned of terrible losses of Allied planes and civilians. There is always a price to pay.

One bombing sortie dropped its bombs on the Dutch side of the border instead of on Cleef, the German side. It was a navigational error; 2,000 Dutch civilians were killed and the centre of the ancient city destroyed. Each sortie brought thousands of silver strips raining down from the planes, intended to confuse German radar and anti-aircraft guns.

Early one afternoon after a session playing with the Haarlem kids, I went back to finish my quota of log sawing. I stopped in mid-stroke when I saw a dark-brown Ford hurtling down the lane leading to our entrance. It braked hard when it reached our driveway. I was at the back of the house shielded from view, so I immediately went to Henny and Meta's open window and told them about the car. I had no idea who had come, but my gut told me there could be trouble.

I took off full tilt back to my log pile. I skidded around the corner of the house and all but slammed into a man coming the other way. His black suit and matching fedora was a uniform the population had come to know. I gave the Gestapo agent a very polite, "Good afternoon, Sir." Fedora hat brusquely asked in Dutch "And who are you, boy?" My first thought was how shocking that a Dutchman was aiding the Gestapo. Without missing a beat I replied, "I'm Jan van Renkem from Haarlem, and I'm on holiday with my parents." Pointing to one of the cottages, I added, "We're staying over there."

"You have wasted enough of my time kid, buzz off!"

I nonchalantly walked back to the Haarlem kids still playing in the sandpit. I told them as simply as I could if a man in black came asking about me, tell him I am your brother. The kids had no idea what was happening and could not grasp what I was asking. I tried a few more times, but in the end I told them to quit with the questions.

Out of the corner of my eye I saw Henny leave the house. She must have decided to make a run for it through the kitchen exit after she heard the Gestapo fellow questioning me. I was aghast. Animal fear contorted her face as she rushed in my direction. The man in the Fedora had seen her too.

"Hey miss, don't run away, just wait for me!" My heart sank. She was terrified but she stopped on his command. Somehow she regained her composure as he grabbed her arm and dragged her back into the house. I chose this moment to dive into the bush a few metres from the sandpit. I kept myself hidden until nothing else seemed to be happening.

The kids had watched the whole performance from the sandpit. Not one of them whimpered or cried out. Now even children were used to the dramas occupation had imposed on daily life.

After Henny was dragged back to the house, the Gestapo agent told her he was looking for a terrorist. Her heart must have skipped when he said, "But when I see you run away, young lady, I wonder if you are by any chance Jewish." Henny hadn't had the training Moms gave me on how to lie. She submissively admitted she was.

She was told to pack a few belongings and the agent followed her to the bed-sitting room. The tragedy grew uglier when the man saw Meta. She was ordered without questioning to pack her things too. The girls were marched outside to the waiting car while Chris, Aunt Jo and Rosa stood watching helplessly.

Then another commotion broke out. Uncle Chris was arrested on the spot, along with the pregnant Rosa, the agent all the while screaming, "I hereby charge you with harbouring Jews!" Rosa and Chris were pushed outside to join Meta and Henny in the car. It pulled out of the driveway in a cloud of dust.

Glued to the bushes near the sandbox I did not know what had happened at the house. I tried to dream up schemes to help the girls but could think of nothing practical. I pulled myself together and decided what I would do.

I leapt like a deer deeper into the cover of the young trees and ran for my life. I passed our pup tent, knowing I should deflate and bury it, but I couldn't raise the nerve to stop. I kept running full tilt until I reached the fire lane on the edge of the property. My heart was banging and I saw my arms and legs were scratched and bloody from the undergrowth. My hanky was too small to mop up the bleeding. I was terrified that the Gestapo might have posted lookouts or brought dogs to watch for anyone escaping.

I reasoned that crossing the fire lane might not be a smart idea, so instead I slumped down where I was. Nearly eight hours went by. It was an interminable length of time but I forced myself to be patient until dark, when I stealthily made my way back to the pup tent.

What might have happened at the house gnawed away at my gut, but in exhaustion I just curled up in the tent and fell asleep. There were no passionate prayers from Wim to keep me awake.

Violent scratching seeped into my conscious and I woke in terror. The glittering eyes of a wild cat stared from the tent opening and I let out a mighty howl. The animal sniffed and finally slunk away. I laughed hysterically.

Uncle Carl had given me an old watch, so I knew it was just on nine when the cat had woken me. I was desperate to get back to the house for news. I buried the tent and crept along the fire lane to about 500 metres from the back yard. I saw Aunt Jo in the distance, probably looking for me. At that moment, we were both distracted by a loud noise overhead. The sky was suddenly full of the contrails of a thousand Allied bomber planes droning through the sky. The noise was phenomenal and all thought of catching Aunt Jo's attention went out of the window. I tried to imagine the organization it needed to get a thousand Allied planes in the air for bombing raids.

Eventually Aunt Jo caught sight of me and rushed over smothering me with kisses and embraces. Over and over she kept thanking the Lord for saving me then said, "Now it will be possible to give you back to your father when the war ends!"

She became subdued as she told me about the raid. I could see horror in her eyes and her voice quavered as she told of the Gestapo taking Chris and Rosa, along with my cousins. Fortunately *Zwarte* Gert and Jan had been away from the house during the raid. Wim had left the van Schuppen place a few days earlier and no one knew where he had gone. No one asked.

Aunt Jo had realized the Gestapo visitors were looking for Wim. The Germans were furious that the terrorist, as they called him, had done so much damage to their vital Luftwaffe air base at Soesterberg.

Distraught as she was, Aunt Jo had kept her wits about her during the raid and heard the driver being instructed to head first for Elisabeth Homestead in case Wim might have fled there. I had visions of the agents pulling on Nel's hair, and I especially visualised the wild protests Liesje would make. Then it struck me the Gestapo was getting very accurate in its searches when it could zero in on the Homestead and the van Schuppen house. Access to both places involved driving through winding roads deep in the woods. "The Gestapo must have an informer in the area," I thought to myself.

Aunt Jo took me inside and I was shocked by the deathly quiet pervading the usually bustling house. She realized I hadn't eaten for twenty-four hours and she watched me gulp down the rich farm milk and omelette she had rustled up. A wave of nausea came over me and I had to stop eating. Nervous tension from the devastating raid was taking over from the adrenalin that had carried me through. I simply could not take in the fact that Henny and Meta were gone.

Thankfully, Rosa was released within a few days. There was no sign of Chris or my dear cousins. They were being held at the Scheveningen prison, which had come to be called the Orange Hotel.

Rosa filled us in, bit by bit, on what happened to her. They did indeed first drive to Elisabeth Homestead and two of the Gestapo police leapt out and hammered on the front door. It took a long time before the ladies opened up. The agents pushed past Aunt Johanna and went into the house, having left the driver, with gun in hand, to guard the prisoners. The two agents returned after a short time empty handed. They must have been convinced Wim wasn't there.

The car set off and before they even reached the Orange Hotel, Henny and Meta had been made to give up their watches and rings. "You won't need your jewellery where you are going," one of the men had told them.

Chris van Schuppen, after two weeks of gruelling interrogation, was released from the Orange Hotel hell hole. He was a limp rag, but alive. He had been able to convince the interrogators he had not known Meta and Henny were Jewish and that he certainly was not hiding anyone. The slightest taint of Resistance involvement meant execution or prison. Many of Holland's finest citizens never came out of the Orange hotel. Jews were automatically sent on to the Westerbork deportation camp.

After all the uproar Aunt Jo turned her attention to me. She felt her home was no longer safe and had arranged for a local farmer to keep me while her Resistance contacts looked for a new family to hide me. I was told to go to the vicinity of my pup tent when it got dark and wait for the farmer to collect me.

I got there about eleven. I huddled close to a young fir tree in pitch dark waiting for the farmer. I got colder by the minute. I fretted about whether something had gone wrong. Nearly an hour passed and nobody appeared. I felt there must be trouble so moved even deeper into the woods. "The Gestapo must have come back to smell out any hiders who had returned after the raid," I thought to myself, fearing I would soon be discovered.

Finally, when it was well past midnight, I decided to go back to the house. I gave my lovely Aunt Jo a fright when I woke her, but she hugged me and rustled up a welcome snack. As she took me up to a bedroom, I heard her muttering, "How can a child bear so much?" She fell on her knees by my bed and prayed with as deep a passion as Wim's. With my last strength I listened and drifted off to sleep. I, too, had learned to be comforted by prayer.

Next morning Aunt Jo took me a kilometre through the bush to the farmer who was supposed to have met me. Before she left I got my usual big hug but this time with a surprise gift. She handed me a large illustrated children's Bible, so now I owned two.

Aunt Jo came back the next day with news; she had been directed by the Resistance to take me in a few days to an abandoned poultry coop close by. I was to stay with a Jewish father and son who had agreed to let me join them in hiding. Aunt Jo had noticed the dilapidated poultry pen earlier but was not sure if it was good enough to house people. Like it or not, the poultry pen would be my new home. I would no longer have a mom.

Commentary

It was a huge coincidence that I should have met Wim. I had felt the explosion from Soesterberg while I was in a small fishing village with Uncle Willem during one of our selling trips. We were terrified and could not imagine what might have caused it. News got around days later that the munitions depot at the air base had exploded into the sky. I never imagined I would one day meet the perpetrator.

CHAPTER 8

JOURNEY TO DEATH

It is impossible to know exactly what happened to Henny and Meta after they were separated from Rosa and Chris, but between Herman's account of his visit to the camp, and reading about the fate of others sent from Westerbork to Auschwitz, I pieced together a basic scenario. My imagination filled in the dreadful details.

After being driven for nearly two hours, the girls reached the Orange Hotel. They had heard of this dreadful and feared prison located at Scheveningen. Many Resistance people were held there, tortured and shot. Some prisoners found themselves transported to forced labour camps in Germany and Poland.

The girls were immediately separated from Rosa and Chris van Schuppen and taken to an interrogation room. Henny and Meta had not practised the art of lying, but they had gone over their cover story a million times, sometimes with me pretending to be the interrogator. The scenario was that they were students at the universities of Utrecht and Amsterdam taking a break in the countryside to study for their doctoral exams. We three had also rehearsed the story in front of the van Schuppens, so the girls were not worried that Chris or Rosa would give conflicting stories.

A bureaucrat sat at the desk, but they were left standing. He painstakingly wrote down all their details in a register and then he commenced his terror tactics. The girls sensed he was suspicious of Resistance activity at the van Schuppen home because he demanded to know the minutest details of how they had ended up there.

As planned, Henny told the interrogator they were staying at the van Schuppen's for a few weeks because they needed a quiet place to study for their upcoming exams. She explained they had not known the van Schuppens; a university friend had told them the couple took in summer and other paying guests. She bravely insisted that no one at the van Schuppens knew they were Jewish.

Despite her confidence, the interrogator stormed back that she was lying. He told her curtly they would be sent to the Westerbork deportation camp the next day. The girls were distraught and close to collapse as they were marched back to their cell and pushed in like cattle.

The interrogator's orders were carried out and they left the Orange Hotel the next day in a van. They arrived at the transport camp, a hell hole with thousands of people milling around. Meta and Henny were checked in at the entrance office. They had no valuables left but others around them were made to give in watches and rings. The girls were led from the office to one of the sparse stone barracks dotted around the camp. They found women and children jammed together stretched out on foul smelling wooden bunks covered with filthy straw. The place was crawling with insects, which caused unbearable itching. Hell enveloped them.

There was nerve wracking tension in the air as each inmate awaited the Monday roll call of names selected for the next day's transport. There was nothing haphazard or random when the selection lists were prepared to meet the weekly quotas. Every name and detail was meticulously recorded. Nobody was missed. Only German Jewish refugees got some reprieve by helping the administration prepare the weekly selections. The guards went to each bunkhouse Monday evening to read the chosen names. Those called were told to pack their belongings for departure next morning. Those not called speculated they might live until the following week's train. Each day of the week passed in mounting terror.

Meta and Henny were shocked to find themselves on the list their very first Monday at the camp. The chosen were dragged and prodded out of the barracks early Tuesday morning. Meta, Henny and the others destined for the train siding waited outside in a forlorn group.

The ritual at Westerbork was for a train to leave each Tuesday with one to two thousand inmates bound for a concentration camp. Most suspected this meant imminent death. The names of Auschwitz and Bergen-Belsen entered the camp vocabulary, and later Mauthausen, Sobibor and Theresienstadt.

The girls were moved out so quickly because they had consciously hidden from the Germans as opposed to being rounded up. The ragged group culled from their barracks was marched to the train siding on the camp perimeter. No passenger trains awaited; they could hardly believe their eyes when they saw a long line of cattle cars with sliding doors.

There was hardly room on the platform for those congregated. The mass of humanity included really old people and crying newborns, as well as adults and children. The very weak and sick were transported to the sidings in carts pushed by young boys. They unceremoniously dropped their barely live cargos, wheeled around, and went back for more.

Guards and fierce dogs patrolled up and down the platforms squelching anyone's idea of making a run for it. The loading began and prisoners were packed so tightly there was no room to lie down. Meta and Henny leaned against each other for support, continually retching from the smell of the fouled straw scattered over the floor boards. When loading was complete, doors clanged shut and the train whistle blew.

Once rolling, the grim reality of their situation hit the passengers. The toilet was a wooden barrel placed in the corner of the car. Hours passed and no food or water appeared. It was August, and it was sweltering inside the cattle car. There was no ventilation except through broken slats in the walls.

Normally, the journey from Westerbork to Auschwitz took less than two days, but the human cargo trains were given low priority and often stood for hours on sidings. It is possible that the train the girls were on took five days to reach Auschwitz. Few babies or elderly survived the ordeal.

The train pulled into the Auschwitz camp siding and all passengers, living and dead, were shoved out. Those still standing were lined up under the eyes of SS guards and fierce, growling dogs. Camp personnel in white coats, perhaps doctors, sat at tables interviewing the passengers as they shuffled by.

The exhausted travellers were channelled into two groups. One was for those who appeared fit and capable of work. The other was for the debilitated. Many women, and all children, were being directed to the second group. Henny and Meta, terrorized for days and weakened by the journey, easily fell into the latter group. Along with the other petrified victims, they went on a slow, bedraggled trek to the shower buildings. They were told to undress and line up to go into the showers. Mothers, hardly able to cope with themselves, awkwardly undressed their crying children.

The naked Enemies of State, along with hundreds of others, were herded into the shower building. They heard the showerheads gurgling, but gas, not water, came hissing out. Like a huge wave, the prisoners began clawing one another trying to escape the poisonous air. One by one the victims collapsed and blacked out. It had been barely two weeks since Henny and Meta were forced from the van Schuppen home; now they lay dead amid a sea of bodies.

Two fine young women, amiable, educated, and in love with life perished at the hand of state-sanctioned mass murder.

Their names, along with the date of their death at Auschwitz — September 3th, 1943 — were among the thousands of others listed in the pages of *In Memoriam,* a register of more than 100,000 Dutch Jews who perished in the Holocaust.

If my cousins had not been forced to leave Westerbork so quickly, they might not have suffered this fate. The day they were caught, Aunt Jo got word of the arrest to Uncle Willem via the Resistance. He and Aunt Eva, who were also in hiding, told their contact to ask Henny's fiancé to go to camp Westerbork. Herman was authorized to offer whatever amount was demanded to obtain the girls' release.

Herman knew he was putting himself at risk by trying to negotiate a release, but he went willingly. He spoke fluent German and quickly gained an interview with Commandant Gemmecker. Despite the human hell hole Herman saw around him in Westerbork, the commandant was able to obtain in short order meticulous records of the girls' prison status.

The young man was stunned when he learned Meta and Henny had already been sent to Auschwitz. Distraught, he was ushered out of the office and escorted to the camp gates. He leaned against the railings, trembling. He didn't know how he would find the strength to break the dreadful news to Willem and Eva.

Another young man was also heart broken when the girls were arrested. I knew little about it, but a romance had bloomed between Jo's cousin and Meta.

Commentary

Dutch railroad workers went on strike to protest the loading of Jews onto the trains destined for the camps, but dozens of these men were shot on the spot to discourage further disobedience.

A controversy still rages on the pages of history as to why the transport train rail lines, and the camps themselves, were not precision bombed by the

Allies, or sabotaged more by the Resistance. The violent persecution of the Jews and other minorities, and the existence of the extermination camps, was certainly known to the Allied high command in Washington and London; yet, no precision bombing was ever planned to alleviate the situation. Such bombing would have kept a few planes out of the regular bombing, and many in the trains and camps might have been killed, too, but surely such acts would have slowed down the death production lines. The Germans always did their best to disguise their activities, which tells me they knew their actions were unacceptable to the outside world. What sane person could have believed what was going on in the camps? The horror was not generally revealed until the gates were opened towards the end of the war.

The task of trying to save the persecuted was left in the hands of those brave few who arranged hiding places, and to the families who opened their homes as sanctuaries. Sadly, they could not save millions. I believe only the leaders of Denmark and Bulgaria offered state sanctioned help to Jews.

The van Schuppen home housed many memories that would follow me for life. I could never ever forget Wim, who used to exhort me to join his impassioned prayers. I still can hardly believe this man was the terrorist he was claimed to be. He survived the war and joined the Dutch military as an officer. On his way to the then-Dutch East Indies, authorities came aboard his ship and arrested him on the charge of treason. I have never been able to locate any records of his trial, but I plan to continue my investigations. I suspect he may have been a double agent. This mysterious individual had played a dangerous game.

Whatever his virtues or vices, I can never forget the Gestapo would not have come to the van Schuppen house if they had not been looking for Wim. My dear cousins had been caught in his web.

CHAPTER 9

THE POULTRY PALACE

During the few days I spent with the farmer and his wife, I occupied most of my time studying the children's Bible Aunt Jo had given me. In the back of my head I was worrying about what might have happened to Meta and Henny, and I was afraid I would be the next to be rounded up. Because this farm was so close to the van Schuppens, I couldn't help feeling it, too, would be kept under surveillance.

I hardly got to know the farmer's wife, but just the same I relished her, knowing there would be no woman at the chicken barn. After three days I was bundled up, given lots of sandwiches, and told to meet Aunt Jo at the end of the pathway. It was eerily silent in the lush surrounding bush and I was glad she took my hand as we began our short journey. We walked about half a kilometre, first doubling back past the farm, then going in the opposite direction. When we first saw the dilapidated chicken pen, my heart sank.

The old, ramshackle building had probably been built as a shed. There was not a grain of paint left on it and the wood had weathered badly. The structure looked as though it was about to fall apart. I rationalized it would make a good hiding spot. After all, who would think humans could live in there?

We were expected; just the same my polite Aunt Jo tapped on the rickety door before gingerly pushing it open. "Here's Pieter," she announced. I saw two pale, long haired males who looked as though they had escaped from a Borneo jungle. Guessing their ages was hard, but the father was about forty and the son perhaps thirteen. I was glad I would have someone close to my age to talk to.

Aunt Jo bade me goodbye with copious amounts of her usual passion. She admonished the two occupants to take good care of me because she now had few left that were dear to her. In a torrent of tears, she retold the story of how her husband and pregnant daughter in law had been taken in the raid along with my cousins. Her final farewell was, "May my good Lord be with you during these terrible times."

The minute Aunt Jo left, the father introduced himself as Jos and announced clearly, "From now on Pieter you will only whisper. Survival depends on not being heard by neighbours or strangers." He offered an upturned crate and I sat myself down with the little suitcase at my side wondering what to do next. I sensed Jos and his son, Lo, were wondering what kind of a boy I was. All I could think of was that for a sickly looking young fellow, Lo was named after a very grand person: Lodewijk, Napoleon's brother, who had governed Holland in the early eighteen hundreds.

During those strange, uncomfortable first few days, I thought deeply about my life on the run. I had been in hiding for just over a year, had moved nine times, and had come dangerously close to being captured. I had been lucky. I realized I was slowly coming out of the stunned state that had enveloped me since the Nazi raid. I refused to allow myself to dwell on what I had just lost — my cousins, glorious farm food, and the freedom of running around outside. Instead, I concentrated on making the best of things. My world now consisted of this six by fourteen metre wooden shack, two silent strangers and a few chickens. But, I was alive!

Thankfully, Jos and Lo warmed up to me within a few days; after all, what else could we do but get along with one another. Pretty soon I was calling him Uncle Jos, and he didn't seem to mind. I started reading the children's Bible to them although they frequently had to remind me to speak softly. I was surprised how intently they both listened and I think we all got some satisfaction out of the words.

However, it was not solemn words that helped us stay sane. It was gallows humour. We three chicken coop guys became very adept at this form of wit. Our continual good humour meant there was no arguing, fighting, or bad temper. I was soon cackling about everything. We nearly killed ourselves trying to laugh silently. Pretty soon I was indoctrinated into their way of life and could keep up with the fast-paced funereal joking.

Our constant quest was to make our palace look as though it was still a real poultry house, so we always had a few charming chickens running around our feet. Jos and Lo concocted a rough, wooden bed frame for us three. It was covered with straw, so naturally the chickens liked it, too, frequently laying their eggs all over the bed. We forever tried to imitate the chickens clucking away, at the same time giggling and worrying that the cock would come after us. The chickens had a bad habit of scraping for worms in our smooth floor so it was hard for us to keep it tidy. To me the chickens had an arrogant air but I suppose we humans were no better or worse; we both arose and went to bed at the same times.

We lived in our palace under the benevolent protection of the Hendriksen family and we were careful to turn all the eggs over to them. The Hendriksens sold them at hefty prices on the black market and Uncle Jos penned a poem declaring, "The chicken and the Jew, together provide the stew."

Just about all families who were hiding Jewish people were paid to do so by their relatives or the Resistance groups. The latter organizations, in addition to sabotage duties, developed into highly secret and intricate networks responsible for finding and supervising hiding locations. None of us begrudged the Hendriksens their income, but we would have been overjoyed to eat an extra egg now and again. As the days turned into weeks, I had more than enough time to scrutinise my new sanctuary. Even in the best frame of mind I could only declare our palace was falling apart. There were wide openings between the slats, and the few windows were cracked and so dirty they gave little light. There were decades of dust and dirt caked inside and out, but I supposed it really was the ultimate camouflage for anyone evading detection.

As an outlet for our freedom yearnings we turned the dusty walls into murals. We drew our hopes, and sometimes our nightmares. We even added our own version of the chicken scratches we saw on the earthen floor.

Naturally there was no running water, electricity, or heat but just the same Uncle Jos shaved daily in what was left of the watery coffee. Our toilet was an elegant metal barrel.

The last days of summer disappeared, autumn came and went, and then winter blasted through the walls of our hen house. We couldn't risk smoke curling from our roof so there was no thought of burning logs. We stayed warm wearing many layers of wool, and when we could find the energy we ran on the spot to keep our blood circulating.

During our many hours of whispered conversation, I learned Jos had

had a successful coffee import-export business, which obliged him to travel extensively. He was often in Sweden, France and New York, always taking his actress wife with him. Bit by bit it came out that his marriage had not been very happy. Their daughter was supposedly hiding with her mother, but he had no recent news of them. Uncle Jos had been chased out of many hiding places so his eight-month sojourn at the chicken palace, while not luxurious, was something of a treat. The Resistance had arranged for Lo to join him four months before I arrived on the scene.

We all craved something to occupy us. The Hendriksens had a few sheep, and many tufts of wool were lying around the farm. Uncle Jos persuaded Mrs. Hendriksen to collect the wool and let him use her spinning wheel. Every day he produced wool for her and I know the spinning helped his sanity. He hummed as he worked, quite oblivious to his surroundings. His favourite tunes were "Parlez-moi d'amour" and the "Marseillaise." Lo and I embarrassed him by saying he was as good as Charles Trenet!

Lo's way of keeping busy was to grow beanstalks, which he trained up the cracked windows to try to block the cold drafts. I think he fantasized he was Jack of Jack and the Beanstalk fame, and he expected the giant to come along at any moment to rescue us from our dismal surroundings. They must have been winter beans because they flourished magnificently. As they inched up, Lo was in awe. He was overjoyed that he could add a few centimetres of nature to our abnormal home. It was a victory of the spirit for him and Uncle Jos, and I participated in their happiness.

My daily duty was to peel the pail of potatoes that Mrs. Hendriksen left religiously at the chicken palace. When Jos and Lo felt magnanimous they took a few turns at the peeling. I ate so many potatoes while at the chicken palace I couldn't stand them for years after.

Another time-passer was reading the daily fascist newspaper Mr. Hendriksen passed onto us. It did not take much reading between the lines to determine the Germans were controlling the daily press. Uncle Jos and I soon got the hang of interpreting the slanted news that was being put out by Goebbels' ministry of misinformation in Berlin.

Despite our ingenious attempts to keep busy, time passed slowly, and our thoughts were always turning to food. Theus and Betty Hendriksen risked their lives for us but were simply unable to provide enough food. Their house was pretty close to the highway but three times a day they invisibly managed to bring us meagre meals and the other bare necessities. During that winter of

1943, food became scarcer. Our daily rations were small but the general Dutch population was not faring much better.

Breakfast was two slices of bread each, and pretty quickly I began to get used to the soft pulp that during the war passed for bread. The weak coffee, as Uncle Jos had found, was better suited to shaving water. The coffee constantly broke his heart when he remembered the strong brews of his business days, but he never complained.

Our daily lunch was not much more exciting. Accompanying another two slices of bread, we sometimes got butter or margarine, and once a week we were spoiled rotten with a thin cheese slice or a boiled egg.

We learned to look forward to dinner, which generally arrived as a mound of vegetables and lots of potatoes. We would poke around and with great delight fish out minute bits of meat or the odd chicken bone. We reflected on how our lives had changed when it took only a few morsels of chicken to make us happy. Miraculously, we didn't get sick or even catch cold from our reduced diet or the unhygienic conditions. The Hendriksens gave us quinine pills which we took daily; we thought they were only for malaria but they seemed to protect us.

I turned thirteen while at the chicken palace, and my teenage appetite grew apace with my years. Both Lo and I were hungry most of the time. Uncle Jos would sometimes give Lo or me his entire ration when he sensed we were close to breaking down from hunger. I had the idea Uncle Jos was practising self-hypnosis, and that in his mind he was in Paris or Stockholm wildly enjoying himself in a classy restaurant.

We were beginning to think of ourselves as humanoid chickens but this did not dampen our desire to celebrate our birthdays, St. Nicholaas Day, or any Allied victories we learned about, whether they be in Russia or North Africa. It was an especial treat when for about thirty minutes on Christmas Day the Hendriksens came over to us for a short Holy Day celebration.

An onlooker might have thought these celebrations were sad little affairs but we enjoyed them as much as being at the Ritz. At one point we turned the palace into a makeshift casino and games room. We hung black sheets to cordon off an area by the slatted wall and set out four fruit crates to form the gambling table. We begged a few more boxes from the Hendriksens to use as seats. Before we started rolling the dice, we put rags on the table to dampen the sound.

We had a huge games repertoire and played chess, drafts, Monopoly and some obscure board game called Variety. We used a few precious candles to give light and some warmth. We chattered and cackled away, continually admonishing each other to keep the noise down. We played late into the night, accompanied by the sweet music of Allied planes humming overhead on yet another raid into Germany.

It wasn't easy, but we saved apples, carrots and other morsels from our already thin meals to eat in the evening while we played. Uncle Jos's thrill was to smoke an ersatz cigar that Mr. Hendriksen obtained using Jos's illegal ration card. These ration cards and other identification documents came from raids the Resistance guys made on town hall offices.

Interspersed with these sweet moments were visits from unwelcome guests. We were inundated with mice, which were never shy. They were cheeky enough to run over our feet, hands and faces as we slept. We would slap them away or crush them and we started mice catching competitions. I soon became the champion mouse destroyer but my victories were easy because Lo was squeamish and his gentle soul refused to kill anything. A pest, mouse, bee, or fly that buzzed around him was perfectly safe.

I kept my brain busy writing a diary and faithfully buried it under the straw-covered bed planks. My aim was to record not only day-to-day facts, but our moods. I took pains to describe the goodwill shown in the chicken coop because I believed such civility strengthened our spirits and went a long way to helping us cope. The weather deeply affected our moods and each degree falling below zero brought on more discomfort. Food, or the lack of it, also dramatically dictated our mood. We sought to keep our appearance normal, but trying to be barbers with scissors which had half a blade on one side produced fits of giggles. We managed to keep ourselves reasonably clean with the one pail of warm water Mrs. Hendriksen brought us daily. Sometimes we used the same water to do our laundry.

We did not deceive ourselves that life in the chicken palace was all fun and games. Uncle Jos had a revolver and he demonstrated how he would use it if we were raided. He had thought out an escape procedure. He explained how he would cover us boys while we slipped through the boarded up hole that served as our rickety back door. Under the cover of darkness, we rehearsed this manoeuvre a hundred times. Once outside, we headed for the woods in a direct line behind the chicken coop. Our escape scheme was dissected and practised to perfection. Somehow having these plans in place did a lot for our self confidence.

In the end we didn't have to use our meticulous escape plan. But we did have to leave in a hurry. One stark, cold afternoon in January 1944, our front door was wrenched open. We three must have looked like rabbits caught in headlights. It was too late to get out the gun or run.

We always had our ears trained to the ground, but we hadn't heard a thing. A tall man peered inside and took in the scene. He obviously grasped we were in hiding. "Good afternoon, people, please don't let me worry you," he said quickly. In his haste to leave, he slammed the door so hard the whole chicken coop shook. We thought he was heading for the Hendriksen's house, but he veered away and ran out of the yard.

Uncle Jos's first reaction was that we had been betrayed, but it came to Lo that he had seen the tall fellow before when hiding in another village. He told us the villagers had suspected this man of being a spy. We knew reinforcements would be back to arrest us.

Uncle Jos rushed over to the Hendriksens and told them we were leaving immediately. Theus Hendriksen, in his calm way, phoned his Resistance contact and obtained emergency instructions. Lo and I were directed to walk separately to a certain fashion store in Lunteren about ten kilometres away. We were to stay there the night and wait for news from Uncle Carl. It was many years before I learned where Uncle Jos went.

Contacting Resistance members was always dangerous, so all kinds of ruses and codes were dreamed up. Uncle Carl was still under constant surveillance and his phone was bugged. The safest route for messages was via bicycle couriers. Resistance people devised communication codes that allowed verbal messages to be passed in the open at sporting activities or at church meetings. The Lunteren fashion shop owners we were heading to usually used a phone code saying a dress was either ready or that the customer needed to come in for another fitting.

Lo and I had raced out of the chicken palace with little more than we were wearing. I didn't remember grabbing it, but I was happy to find my toothbrush in my pocket. We went over and over what or who might have revealed our hiding spot. It could have been a local baker or grocer who noticed the Hendriksens buying more food than was necessary or using extra ration cards. Or it could have been someone just desperate to feed his family. Dutch citizens could earn ten dollars for reporting Jews in hiding. Rabbits cost thirty dollars at the butchers.

I separated from Lo and headed for the dress shop via a quiet, little-known avenue with almost no traffic. "Thank goodness Uncle Jos cut my hair a few days earlier and I'm looking tidy for a change," I thought to myself. I was covering a lot of ground, forcing a jaunty whistle, when out of the blue a cyclist came towards me. I was breathing fast and my stomach really churned when I saw he wore a black Dutch Nazi uniform. He could not fail to notice me; I was the only pedestrian in sight.

Just the same, my old survival instinct clicked in and I nodded to the cyclist. He kept going and I didn't look back at him. "I'm going to be lucky again. I'm going to be lucky again," I chanted. I moved on, praying for some protective hand to stay over my head. I began feeling cold, probably from anxiety as much as from lack of warm clothing. I pushed myself to keep going.

I found the shop easily and saw there was an owner's residence on the upper floors. My new Mom, Mrs van Schuppen, was a relative of the other van Schuppens I had stayed with. She ushered me into the hallway and told me Lo had already arrived. He was sprawled on one of the hall benches, obviously as exhausted as I was. She took us upstairs, sat us down, and barraged us with questions about where we were from and what we had been through. Suddenly I began laughing hysterically as I tried to tell the poor woman I had been leading the life of a chicken. Mrs. van Schuppen and Lo looked concerned. Obviously, I was suffering a nervous reaction. As the evening wore on I calmed down.

Mrs. van Schuppen finally heard that Uncle Carl would pick me up next morning and somebody else would collect Lo. Our temporary mom gave us a really decent dinner, and we relished every last bite. As we started to eat Lo had put a finger over his lips and I realized I had been shouting. After four months of enforced whispering, I seemed to have forgotten how to speak at a normal level.

My new mom explained that although they were related to the other van Schuppens, she and her husband had no active role in the Resistance except to quietly help in times of emergency. She said many more people were now willing to do this; the longer the occupation dragged on, the more the Dutch hated their Nazi masters. The few hours we stayed at the van Schuppens seemed surreal. In the morning, Lo and I were allowed to wallow in a huge bathtub and we continually swirled hot water over ourselves. Being able to step onto a tiled floor and look into a decent mirror in bright light was almost too much excitement for us. Our hostess had scrounged us new clothes, which we put on with shouts of delight. Then we devoured a marvellous country-style breakfast with lots of eggs and bacon. We ate till we were stuffed.

The Van Schuppens were fascinated by our lives in the chicken palace and asked a million more questions. They never revealed any specific information but we deduced lots of people were being hidden in the surrounding villages.

We jumped at a loud knocking; it was Uncle Carl come to collect me. I was happy and relieved to see him again. After thanking and embracing Mom and her husband, and wishing Lo good luck, I climbed into the waiting car.

"You're very jittery, young man," Uncle Carl remarked straight away, and I realized it was going to take more than the pleasant short stay at the van Schuppens to return me to normal. Uncle Carl was aware of what I had gone through since we last met and understood my condition. "I'll look for a quiet place where you can recover from this trauma. In the meantime you can rest at my home for a few days. But you must be careful; we are still being watched," he said with a resigned smile. My heart leapt at the thought of seeing the kind aunts again in their grand home.

Commentary

In the "phony war" period before hostilities started, the Dutch government, preparing for the worse, stocked up on what they thought was a five year's supply of food for the nation. They did not reckon on the marauding nature of the invader; it took the Germans a little over one year to plunder this food cache. Dutch people would look on with disbelief when they saw soldiers walking the streets laden down with food parcels destined for their deprived families in Germany. Most forgot Germany had been on a wartime footing since 1933 when Hitler had offered "butter or guns." They had screamed in massive, hysterical unison "GUNS" and there had been hardships ever since.

I went back to the Hendriksens after the war. While talking about our dramatic escape from the chicken coop, I asked Mrs. Hendriksen whether she had found my diary. In my haste to escape, I had left it buried under the straw. She could not recall the diary, but said she would have burned it along with everything else we left behind.

Lo and I applied to have Mrs. Hendriksen honoured by the Israeli Yad Vashem Memorial. She was inducted at a Righteous Among the Nations ceremony hosted by the Israeli Ambassador in Amsterdam in December 1983. Theus Hendriksen had died earlier in a flash flood in Australia. The couple had planned to emigrate.

I would have proposed many of the other people who had so bravely given me sanctuary, but it just was not possible to do this from Canada.

*Fred age 12 at Elisabeth
Homestead*

Fred with Johanna's dog

*Chris van Schuppen during
the war*

The Poultry Palace

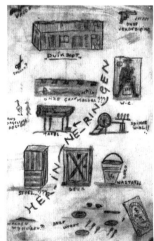

*Fred's drawing of the
chicken coop amenities*

CHAPTER 10

WOOD CHOPPERS FROM GOD

After a few glorious days of luxury living, it was time to move on. Uncle Carl checked that the coast was clear then we ran from his front door and jumped into the car. As we drove off, we scanned the road behind us. We were not being followed.

"The Jansens are certainly not well off," he said as we drove to my next refuge, but they are among the most industrious people I have ever met." He then went on to tell me I was to continue using my old cover name, Pieter van Katwijk. Some Resistance records had gone missing and they were trying to be ultra cautious. I asked if the new Jansens were related to the wonderful family with the tiny house in Terschuur. Carl said they weren't. Anyway, those people had spelled Janssen with a double s.

Within thirty minutes, we had pulled up at the Jansen's modest duplex and hurried inside. Uncle Carl introduced me as Pieter and left quickly.

Mr. Jansen was huge; a tall, wide giant with deep crevices in his face. His rough-hewn head looked to me like a sculpture. His main occupation was wood chopping, but both he and his father were forest wardens in charge of the nearby Doorwerth Woods. He had to endure all kinds of weather but at least his activities were spent in the fresh air.

He was a deeply religious man who had no doubts whatsoever about God's word in the Old and New Testaments. I watched with fascination as he prayed both before and after meals, his head shaking up and down. His words were as passionate as a soldier's on the eve of battle. The intensity rose from the depths of his heart and found its way out of this tree of a man as softly and as poignantly as a small child saying his prayers.

Mrs. Jansen, like most of my other moms, was hard working and trying to run a household on insufficient money. A haggard look etched her young face, but just the same she was cheerful and even jolly saying, "My Lord doesn't allow me the luxury of dissatisfaction." She had few earthly possessions but happily shared everything. I could always count on Mom for a sympathetic glance or goodnight hug.

The Jansens were private, shy people and kept their emotions to themselves. It took a good few weeks for them to open their inner feelings, but bit by bit they revealed their day-to-day problems and family secrets. They maintained a very full family life and took us underground guests in their stride as if we were long-time friends.

This was a home with a happy ambience, and as I studied the four Jansen children I saw each was a miniature example of the loving parents. Everyone in this family was affectionate and had a heart of gold. They were a harmonious unit; I didn't hear angry words or see harsh discipline. I came to adore these God fearing people who, like the others who had taken me in, considered it their duty to hide me and provide daily needs. I was treated no differently than the rest of the family and I wrapped myself in the warmth and care of my lovely new mom. Once again, for safety, I had to sleep outside. It was February, but I managed to stay warm because my three-metre-deep dugout was well insulated. It was covered by a canopy of tree branches supposedly awaiting the saw. I was never allowed to go off to bed hungry or cold. Mom made sure I had a huge bowl of hot porridge before heading outside.

Mr. Jansen's parents lived in the other side of the duplex. I rarely went there but I soon discovered the senior Jansens were hiding three adults. Once these undergrounders trusted me they told me their histories. Each had his unique horror story. Leo had been hiding separately from his wife and two daughters and was in a constant state of nervous tension worrying about their welfare, even imagining they were dead. The second man, Henk, was a teacher from Nijmegen, destined for forced labour in Germany. He told me he was not inclined to support the German war effort and had contacted the Resistance for a hiding place.

The last hider, Max, was the bane of my life. He was a tall, heavy kid from Amsterdam, two or three years older than I was. He was every inch a bully. He sized me up as a good target; after all I was younger and smaller. He pestered me with vicious kicks and cuffs around my ears, which always happened when nobody else was around. It was my bad luck that the family had sent him to share my sleeping hole and he continued his daytime jabbing when he came to bed. My nerves were still unsteady, so Max's constant torment was almost more than I could stand. During his regular brief visits, Uncle Carl could see I was on edge. He thought smoking would calm me so began bringing me cigarettes. Before long I was smoking twenty a day.

Inevitably, Max jabbed me once too often, and with much bravado I challenged him to a fight. Henk agreed to act as the referee. The rules were set at no scratching, no kicking and no punching below the belt. Knowing I was up against a much bigger boy, I set about devising a strategy to beat him. The minute the contest started I grabbed his legs and pulled him to the ground; he didn't know what hit him! Once down we attacked each other ferociously, but I concentrated on keeping him on his back. With that advantage I continually got in good blows, and even I was surprised at the real beating I gave him. When his face was all bloodied and he could no longer see me, he screamed for a truce.

He never bullied me again. As it turned out, he had a chance to get even with me a few months later. To his credit, and my great relief, he didn't.

I told Uncle Carl about the fight on his next visit. He laughed his head off and quietly said "I don't blame you a bit Fred, the Germans had better look out!" He checked up on me every few weeks and I really enjoyed his surprise visits. We usually found a quiet bench in the yard and discussed the war and the challenges of his Resistance work. I was secretly thrilled that he treated me like an adult. I didn't fool myself that I was a man yet, but I was definitely no longer a child.

He warned me never to hide in a haystack. The Gestapo had found so many people concealed in hay they automatically shot into the stacks and then set them alight. He looked downhearted and this time it was my turn to say I thought he looked jumpy. He explained that the Nazis had stepped up the raids, so more and more undergrounders were being caught. "It's getting increasingly demanding to find families willing to give sanctuary," he said miserably. I silently thanked the gods for the Jansens.

It was easy to settle into the family's cozy routine. I especially enjoyed the evenings. There were plenty of books lying around and I would read while Mrs. Jansen mended her children's clothes. During the day, along with my fellow hiders next door, we peeled potatoes or did whatever chores would help the family. These simple activities took our minds off the always present risk of a Gestapo raid. I was sleeping very well again now that Max had stopped tormenting me and felt comfortable in my cave-like hole in the ground.

Sunday was my favourite day. First there was a special farm breakfast which always meant lots of eggs, bacon, cheese and fresh bread dripping with butter. Then I was ushered to the kitchen annex where three kettles of boiling water stood by the laundry tub. I splashed around and cleaned off a week's accumulation of dirt and dust. Mom Jansen kept my clothes laundered so I was able to change into fresh gear. Then I went back to the table for lots more strong ersatz coffee.

Mrs. Jansen was in a high mood on Sundays. She wore her new coat and paraded around seeking our admiration. The whole family then traipsed out heading for church services. They were a grand little procession.

The Jansen property was not a farm but they grew vegetables and kept a few animals. They also had a large barn where they stored hay and wood. Mr. Jansen's forest warden duties kept him busy mostly thinning out the trees to keep them healthy. While he was working in the woods, I helped with the horse and cow and also tended their few rabbits and chickens. After all I was a chicken expert!

The black and white cat was my favourite member of the menagerie. He didn't have to hunt mice because he had been spoilt rotten by the kids. The cat loved to lick my palm with its rough tongue. I thought only dogs licked humans, but this lovely cat knew I need extra affection. On the other hand, perhaps he just liked the earthy smell that clung to me. I had now been sleeping underground for weeks.

Mr. Jansen taught me and the other undergrounders new skills. I was soon helping him chop wood and could grapple with huge stumps. I learned to stack wood professionally and he promoted me to assembling large loads ready for delivery. Wood chopping really is a splendid occupation and filled a great part of my days. It meant I was always outside in fresh air and I grew biceps like coconuts, along with large calluses.

The violent chopping enriched our fantasies and we discussed who would be beheaded that day. Generally it was Hitler, for whom we had a special decapitation which went horizontally and then vertically. Best of all, being outside meant I could keep an eye open for unwanted visitors.

We were all nervous about strangers. Most country children like the

Jansens were taught to be on their guard and to turn away from strangers. Mr. Jansen, similar to Dr. Mettrop, taught his kids to lie easily when a stranger asked questions.

The Jansen's eldest boy was ten, and a carbon copy of his father. He had also inherited his Dad's good character traits. Although he was younger, he became my best friend. I played with him and his three sisters whenever I was not needed for wood chopping. The girls were bright, pretty and well behaved.

I suppose it was a sign of the times that we kids always played some kind of war game. We didn't allow this to stunt our imagination as we devised the most complicated battles and bombardment scenarios, all of which took place on the large kitchen table. Uncle Carl knew about our games and rose to the occasion. He had delivered to the Jansen home a large supply of toy soldiers, tanks, bombs and other war materials. He also sent building kits and we constructed our own Flying Fortresses. I designed a wooden catapult system that pounded heavy pebble mortars onto the battle scene and pretty much brought the war games to a quick close. We all became staunch little militarists and our cause was no different than that of the Allies.

The adults explained to us it was going to take the might of the Americans mixed with the stubborn British Armed Forces, now including Canadians, Australians, New Zealanders, Indians and South Africans, to beat back this so-far-invincible army. Every country yearned to do its share and it was hoped the long suffering Russians would keep up their enormous support.

By the time spring came, my health had improved immensely. I know being in the company of the Jansens and eating their wholesome food had brought about my progress. The violent thoughts and dreams that had swirled around my mind for so long began to fade. I had been having the same dream over and over where I was being hunted down like a wild animal, merely because a Jewish heart beat inside of me.

One bright afternoon in March I was chopping wood and, following my usual practice, scanning the countryside. In the distance I saw a large black car cross the nearest intersection to the farm. "That looks like a Citroen," I said out loud, although no one else was around. I knew the Nazis often used Citroens, so I didn't take my eyes off the car for a second. I almost dropped my axe as I saw it pull up sharply. Four men in dark suits leapt out. They were still a long way off but all four started a kind of a gallop back to the intersection. Without pausing for breath, they turned into the Jansen's lane.

The memory of another woodpile, and another car filled me with dread.

I ignored Uncle Carl's warning about hiding in hay. The barn was the nearest hiding place so I sprinted towards it and dove inside. I raced to the back door, heart thumping. I desperately hoped I would be able to slip out through the door without being seen and make my way to the duplex to raise a warning. The worst happened. The back door was locked on the outside. I was now a prisoner in the barn and could not warn the others without being seen. I peeped out of the barn and saw that the men had covered the final 400 metres to the property and were heading directly for the Jansen senior's side of the duplex

I froze for a moment then came to my senses. I leapt up the loft ladder, pushing it away as I scaled the last rung. I looked out the barn's one and only window. At first I saw nothing and wondered if I was going out of my mind. Then the men came into view as they reached the duplex.

I burrowed deeply into the hay and pulled loose stalks over the entrance to my tunnel. I knew it was a precarious place to hide but at that moment it was the only spot offering any hope of survival. So trained was I in the ways of the Jansen family I tried praying for help. Visions of bayonets and fire floated in and out of my prayers. My stomach, upset from fright, made me pee continuously into the hay. I didn't want to be found with my wallet. I was damned if I was going to let the Gestapo take the few guilders Uncle Carl had given me, so I hid it under the hay. But I held on to my small pocket knife. It was not much of a weapon, but it might come in useful, even save my life.

The entire thirteen years of my existence went through my mind in short, rippling waves. I was afraid the end was in view. I worked myself into a crouched sitting position, soundlessly shivering and contemplating what was coming next.

Hours passed and I heard nothing. I thought it had been about one o'clock when I ran into the barn, but I was not wearing my watch and had lost track of time. It stayed eerily quiet as I saw myself being choked by smoke and roasted by roaring flames. I could not stop these hallucinations. "Why was nobody searching the barn?" I asked myself, "Had I imagined the Citroen?"

Finally, unable to tolerate the deep silence any longer, I worked up the nerve to creep out of my hay tunnel. I made a beeline for the window, tiptoeing like a fairy. Sure enough the car was still parked in the distance near the intersection, but there was no sign of anyone in the yard. At least I was assured that I hadn't imagined the car.

It came back to me that I had put my watch on the ground while chopping wood. I was mad at myself and vowed I would never do that stupid thing again — if I ever got the chance, that is. I felt another hour pass, all the time cursing myself, but there was still no action. The temperature in my hay tunnel was rising by the minute creating my own private hell.

It must have been the devil who made me crawl out of my hole to check on the outside again. The car was still there. Moving like a crab, I crawled back over the loose planks, looking for a gap so I could see through to the main floor of the barn. My desperate need to know what was happening was getting the better of me. I almost laughed out loud when I found a small opening. I bent down and peered through. It was all I could do to stifle the cry that rose up in my throat. I was so dizzy with shock I was afraid I would faint. Fifteen centimetres below was a Brylcreamed head of dark hair. The body attached to this head was draped in a devilish black suit.

Just then a cow started mooing. The man must have prodded the animal and he suddenly began imitating the cow and mooed back. The comical scene made me even more lightheaded and I could hardly stop myself from exploding with laughter. The man was enjoying himself and kept going with his wailing as he matched the cow's moos. I pulled out my penknife. I could easily have plunged it into his skull, but common sense took over and I stayed fixed in my spot. After a minute or so I made an attempt to back away from the gap. Every piece of crackling hay sounded like explosions to me. I froze and held my breath, expecting the man in black to look up at any second. I could almost hear him yelling at me to come down.

I was still holding my breath when I heard the German leave the barn, mooing as he went out. I couldn't believe my good luck. I exhaled, crawled back into my tunnel and lay prostrate until I could get control of my legs. They had turned to rubber. With the immediate danger over, I began imagining I had been discovered and was now in the Citroen on my way to a concentration camp. "It's only a matter of time and my bones will be ground into fertilizer," I was telling myself. That thought bumped me back to earth. I changed tack and began celebrating my splendid good luck at not being caught.

I was still afraid to move, so stayed in my tunnel, straining to hear any sign of life outside. I thought I heard a child crying, but then I realized it was someone calling Pieter-r-r, P i e t e r-r-r, P i e t e r-r-r. The voice came closer to the barn and I was fairly sure it was my fellow hider, the teacher. But I was not going to be tricked. I told myself the Gestapo agent had a gun at his head and was using him to trick me. I remained silent. The seconds ticked by and I found myself shaking with silent laughter. Now I was no better than a cat being called with, "Here Kitty, here Kitty, here Kitty."

The light was fading and it was still unnaturally quiet outside. No barnyard noises. No wood being chopped. There was much to interest the Gestapo in these two households; four of us in hiding and at least two forbidden radios.

Finally, I risked looking out the window again. The car had gone! Relief flooded through me. I guessed it was about half past six. I had been in the barn around six hours. I gingerly dropped down from the loft and limped to my side of the duplex. There was no sign of Mom and Dad Jansen or the kids. Fearing the worst, I dashed out of the empty home and went to the grandparent's side.

As I rushed through the back door I heard wailing. I made my way to the kitchen, where I saw all the Jensens and Henk slumped around the table. My relief at finding them was spoiled by their visible grief. I knew someone must have been taken. The dreadful scene at the van Schuppen's flashed through my mind. Henk was the first to notice me. He put his arm round my shoulders, walked me outside and gave me the bad news; Leo and Max had been arrested. Also, one of the radios had been confiscated.

My sweet mom, in tears, rushed to join us outside. She did her best to explain that her Lord had been unable to protect Max and Leo but was able to save me. "My prayers have worked for you, dear Pieter," she said while hugging me. We found out later that it was the local baker who earned the Gestapo report money. We could not fathom why the grandparents had not been arrested for hiding the unlucky Leo and Max.

The Gestapo had spoken to Henk, but judging him non Jewish they merely told him to report the following day to the Labour Department in Renkum. I never found out what eventually happened to him.

I knew that I would have to move immediately. Within an hour Mr. Jansen had taken me to the house of one of his colleagues. I was to wait there until the Resistance could find me a new hiding place.

Mr. Jansen left quickly and I was given hot, strong coffee and wrapped in warm blankets. I must have been shivering. My temporary mom hardly had the heart to tell me I was to sleep outside in a ditch in the nearby Doorweth woods. They explained it would be much safer than being in the house.

They settled me into the ditch and covered me with branches. I lay staring at the tree tops through the branches, but I was so cold and frightened I could not fall asleep. I suppose I was feeling sorry for myself. I was lonely and felt again like a lost child. But even though the world was rejecting me, I never lost sight of the fact I was alive and grateful for somewhere to hide. I clung to the belief that I was going to survive.

Commentary

Everyone in the household knew Mrs. Jansen made it her business to record little anecdotes about those who passed through both sides of the duplex. I believed she had some premonition that in better times relatives of those who did not survive might come to see her. She wanted to be able to tell them something that might bring comfort. Also, she faithfully labelled and stored anything the undergrounder had left behind so she could give these items to the relatives. After Leo was taken I felt sure he had been put to death in the camps. I often imagined his wife coming back one day to seek news or some small token of him.

Some years after the war Klaas van Houten and I searched for the Jansens, having in mind to recommend them for a decoration from the State of Israel. Unfortunately, we found only row housing in this once countrified spot.

CHAPTER 11

RUNNING AWAY

It was now April and the sleeting rain and cold did their best to make me gloomy. While Uncle Carl drove me to my next refuge, I could not stop wondering whether living in hiding was to be my permanent lot in life. Up to now I had been mostly optimistic that the Allies would win and my life would return to normal. Suddenly I was not so confident. I was sick of feeling miserable, and upset by being wrenched away from people I had grown fond of. I decided from this instant I was not going to allow myself to grow close to my stand-in families. I knew that sooner or later another catastrophe would force me to flee. As it turned out, I did not have to worry about getting close to anyone for a while; I was moved three times during the next few months.

My first stop was with tenant farmers, the van Milligans, who lived only three kilometres from the Jansens; I could even see their place when I climbed a tree. I quite naturally introduced myself to this new family by my cover name, Pieter. It did not take long for me to discover this new location would not provide the happy family environment I had become used to.

My new parents and their adult daughters were decent people who tried to make my stay bearable. But the thirteen-year-old son was a menace. I was initially thrilled they had a boy near my age, but Hemmy turned out to be the town bully and an utter pest. He was even worse than Max. He recognized I was in a vulnerable position and whenever we were together he gave me a quick punch or took advantage of me. He had long, dirty blond hair that fell over his forehead and prevented him from looking anyone in the eye. He would dream up sadistic little tricks, which he thought very funny. I was forever on my guard trying to outsmart him.

Like everybody else I was required to work hard. I was up at six, and after a meagre supper in the evening we were made to go out again and work until sundown. This meant I mostly did not fall into bed until around eleven.

One of my jobs was feeding the pigs; I was able to turn this chore to my advantage. When nobody was looking, I shared Mr. Grunt's swill to ease my hunger. Although we were on a farm, good food did not reach the table. I found myself chatting to the pig, apologizing for taking his food. When I discovered potato peels were full of vitamins, I told him that he had done me a great favour.

I also chopped wood and looked after a hundred rabbits. I was responsible for cleaning the cages and spreading their manure over the fields. As bad luck would have it Hemmy was told to supervise me. He was always demanding I work faster while keeping up a barrage about how efficient the Germans were compared to me. Such pro-enemy views really irritated me. He also insisted the English would never come to liberate Holland.

We boys also had the job of pruning the crowns of the trees so they would fall easier when chopped down. Hemmy, cackling, always made sure he was above me so that when he threw the branches down they would hit me. One day he tried to pee on me as well. If it would not have put his family at risk, I am quite sure he would have betrayed me to the authorities.

Hemmy's taunts became intolerable, so I did something I had vowed never to do. I begged Uncle Carl to find me another home. He was not pleased and again told me it was getting so dangerous to hide people that fewer families were willing to take the risk. I would have to stay put. I went on with the daily routine for a while, but when Hemmy told me I would soon be dead, I decided not to stick around to find out how he meant to do away with me.

I secretly gathered my belongings, stuffed them in my little case and hid it under the bed. After dinner that evening while the others were busy clearing the table, I tied the case to my bike and cycled off. As I pedalled, I thanked my lucky stars that Uncle Carl had stowed my bike in the trunk of his car every time I moved. My plan was to head for his house in Wageningen about fifteen kilometres away; even though I couldn't be sure he would take me in.

It was already getting dark and I was tired from a full day's work. I was still a long way from Wageningen when I realized I was near the house of a dentist

I had been sent to while hiding with the Mettrop family. As I sat having my cracked tooth fixed, I had noticed that the surgery was part of the residence. Now, telling myself that the dentist would not give me away, I plucked up enough courage to knock on his door. My knees shook as I waited for someone to open the door.

The dentist's wife appeared and gave me an astonished look. I quickly mumbled who I was and asked her to contact Uncle Carl. Then she recognized me and to my huge relief I was invited in. She sat me in the hall and went off to tell her husband. Uncle Carl was telephoned. She came back and explained they would put me up for the night and that Carl would come for me the next morning.

Mrs. Dentist, as I thought of her, immediately became my new mom. She prepared a sumptuous meal for us three and over dinner they told me it was lucky that I stopped at their house because the security police had set up their nightly road block a little further down the road. Without a doubt I would have cycled right into it.

Carl was not exactly mad at me, but he was not too happy either. Although he understood my anxiety about being around Hemmy, he said I would have to go back until he could find somewhere else for me. Hemmy was lectured and he promised to behave himself, but a day later the bully was up to his old tricks again.

By some miracle, another home was found for me a week later. It was south of the River Rhine in the Hemmen-Zetten area, which was the heart of the beautiful Betuwe fruit country. This time it was a family called Parlevliet; a retired foreign officer, his wife and grown daughter.

I was joyful at being in a new home. I was well fed and it was an enormous relief to be away from Hemmy, but before long another problem arose. I was shocked and dismayed when the former foreign officer filled my ears with long tirades against Jews. I held my tongue as I listened to his opinion that the Jews were heretics from the true Christian faith and responsible for society's ills. He told me regularly, and with some passion, that the Jews had killed Jesus, and when they weren't killing Jesus they were cheating people. He always ended these lectures by exhorting me to find salvation with Jesus Christ. Uncle Carl was upset when he heard about this; he took pains to tell the officer he had no right to try to indoctrinate me. Amen.

My bedroom was a little room in the attic with a small window. One night I heard the droning of dozens of aircraft engines overhead. I hoped the planes were on their way to bomb Germany, and I rushed to the window and looked out. The sky was lit up from lights and flames. My eyes were soon riveted on one burning four engine bomber. It was flying at roof level. A man, silhouetted against flames, was walking along the wing. It was a terrible sight and I screamed in terror.

I was now thirteen and sprouting up, but by my reaction I suppose I was still just a scared kid. The daughter of the household came to see what was wrong. I received no comfort from her, only an admonition that I had imagined it. I knew better than to complain again to Uncle Carl. However, my spirits abounded with joy when he came unannounced two weeks later to move me to the Bos family just outside a nearby village, Opheusden. I was still south of the River Rhine.

The Bos home was quite a sight. It was probably 1925 vintage and towered three storeys. It had large gardens front and back, and orchards stretched around the perimeter. Johan Bos was an agricultural engineer specializing in fruit experimentation at the nearby Government laboratory in Kesteren. They were a young family with two children, Arie six and Ella nine. Johan was a good man, but he had a vile temper; I was to encounter frequent tension in the household.

Food was not plentiful in this home, but once the fruit ripened, I was allowed to eat my heart out in the orchards. I learned the skill of fruit picking and enjoyed it so much I often cycled to the neighbours to help them bring in the harvests.

I felt very secure in this peaceful area. I was allowed to leave the property to go as far as the outskirts of Opheusden, so I often wandered there when I had finished my chores. In the beginning I got tricky questions from curious farmers en route. There were children around, too, wanting to know all about me, and it wasn't long before I made new friends. I redeveloped my old role of being an orphaned Rotterdammer. My stories about the bombardment and my dead relatives were embellished, polished, and refined; soon all the neighbours knew every last gruesome detail of my young life.

What thrilled me most about my new home was that Jaap Brakel, one of the neighbour boys, became my best friend. I also got along well with his sister Greta. I couldn't wait for every opportunity to cycle over to them.

Whenever the Resistance got wind of threatened Gestapo raids in our area we were warned and, for my protection, Mr. Bos asked Jaap's family to take me for a few nights. The Brakels knew I was an undergrounder and always agreed. They had a very modern house, a splendid example of Bauhaus/De Stijl architecture which my cousins had taught me about. I just loved the glass walls, oblong shapes, and straight lines. Mrs. Brakel proudly told me it had been featured in an architectural magazine and I thought one day I would like to have such a house.

Mr. Brakel, the town secretary, was a well educated fellow and his wife was totally charming. I could see why Jaap and Greta were so interesting. Last but not least each member of the family was a marvellous bridge player. I had learned how to play bridge when staying with my de Vries cousins and the game had become my passion too. Play was fitted in whenever possible, and I think I gave the Brakels a good run for their bridge money. My stays with the Brakels were short, generally a couple of days, but they gave me extra food, and they certainly refreshed my spirit. My bridge playing improved too!

My life in this orchard community continued at a regular, almost banal level, but everything was to change on September 17th.

Commentary

The van Milligan tenant farmers I first stayed with worked one of the largest landholdings in Holland. It was highly mechanized and had a huge barn to store the crops and house the vast number of farm machines. These enormous fields were also to see a greatly increased level of activity when a quarter of the entire fleet of the British Airborne's gliders and paratroopers landed there in preparation for the Arnhem battle.

Hemmy tracked me down years after I had moved to Canada. He wrote that he was ill and very short of money. I promptly sent him a generous cheque but not long afterwards he wrote demanding further funds.

I rekindled my friendship with Jaap Brakel after the war. He led an exciting life, travelling and living all over the world as a KLM manager. His sister Greta did not fare so well. She was caught in a storm while sailing on the IJsselmeer (Zuiderzee) and drowned.

It always intrigued me that Uncle Carl's huge, flashy Packard auto never seemed to attract attention in a time when there were few family cars left on the roads. For some reason I never questioned him on how he was able to obtain the gasoline, or commented it was strange that we never encountered a roadblock when I was in the car. Perhaps he was receiving good intelligence on road conditions, or perhaps he was born under a lucky star.

Chapter 12

The Battle of Arnhem
Day One

September 17th, 1944, was a milepost in my life. It was the first day of the battle of Arnhem; the battle that gave us real hope of liberation. Unwittingly, I found myself with a front row seat to watch the drama unfurl. The Bos's house was on the very edge of the battle. Sensing I was watching history in the making, I made notes on a tiny pad about every daring parachute drop, every thunderous explosion, and every death throe of the downed planes.

That autumn day dawned bright and sunny. I was outside doing my chores when I heard the familiar drone of airplanes. The sound got louder and louder, until I could feel the ground vibrating. This was no ordinary noise. I could hardly believe my eyes when hundreds of fighter planes came over the horizon. Within minutes they had filled the sky, swarming like mad bees. Allied mad bees!

I ran into the house and raced up the three flights of stairs to the roof. Mrs. Bos, already alarmed by the planes, shouted at me to stay downstairs. I ignored her warning. The formations of murderously screaming Spitfires, Typhoons and other fighter planes throbbed their way into my view. Without warning, a Spitfire broke away from a formation. With guns blazing it screamed down towards the trees just across the road from me. It was firing at an emplacement of German machine gunners, spewing their fire up to the planes. One of the German gunners leapt up and ran for his life. He was a lucky fellow; his gun was reduced to a pile of twisted steel but its ammunition supply continued to explode like firecrackers.

We had no idea the German gunners had been hiding so close to the house and I was stunned. They were so well camouflaged none of us had noticed them while going about our work.

I stayed on the rooftop completely transfixed, observing all the drama around me. The ten by eight metre roof was flat and had a sturdy chimney sticking up from the centre, which gave me something to shelter behind, so I felt safe enough. The very close Spitfire attack suddenly brought me to my senses and I hurried back down the stairs. I did not stay for long though; I was unable to resist the lure of this once-in-a-lifetime air show. I realized I was very exposed but it didn't worry me anymore.

Another near-by German unit pounded its 2cm, 4 barrel anti-aircraft guns non-stop at the Allied planes. I worried that it would be impossible for the pilots to avoid these shells. Indeed, it was impossible. The first plane I saw hit, a Mustang, came screaming down about 700 metres away. Already in flames, it crashed and exploded by the River Rhine. The pilot had bailed out quickly and I whooped for joy as I saw him plummet through the air. His parachute opened and he floated down towards the Rhine. I was sickened to see a few moments later his chute floating on the surface. There was no other movement. He must have drowned.

I kept watching the sky as the activity continued full blast. I saw a Typhoon firing its rockets full bore as it dived towards a locomotive stored at the Kesteren station. The engine was utterly destroyed. We already knew that the Allies routinely strafed whole trains aiming to cripple German troop movements, but it was a shock to see it happen.

After it had finished its destructive work, the Typhoon turned on a dime and came blazing towards my roof position. It was still firing its hissing rockets and I was scared silly. With visions of ending up no better than the locomotive, I made a hasty lunge behind the brick chimney.

All this terror left my legs wobbly and I sat for a while leaning against the chimney. I was trying to get my breath back when Jaap appeared. He had seen me on the roof and didn't want to miss out on anything. The minute Jaap saw the swooping Typhoon from this new vantage point he insisted we both go downstairs. "We would be crazy to stay on the roof," he yelled, "the pilots are shooting at anything that moves."

Jaap was definitely shaken up. I thought he was merely scared by being on the roof, but he had just seen the totally destroyed Kesteren locomotive on his way home from an errand. He told me not only had six rockets hit the engine, the Typhoon had also slammed missiles into the surrounding houses, killing the inhabitants. It was the first time Jaap had seen death and destruction.

Despite my friend's pleas, once again I could not tear myself away from all the action, and in the end we both remained on the roof. We were hugely excited; it was hard not to think of it all as a game. We turned to look at four Typhoons attacking a boat on the River Waal to our south. The planes were firing away as they aimed down at the vessel. It was instantly turned into a huge ball of fire. Debris shot in the air and then showered down. The attack struck me as a magnificent sight, and I fantasized that what was left of the wreck would have an eternal grave on the river bottom.

Eventually Jaap had had enough and disappeared downstairs. It was now mid morning and I had been at my roof observation post for two-and-a-half hours. There was no let up in the intensity of the action. I didn't know what to look at first, but a huge group of Lightnings, glinting in the sun, caught my eye. They dived in unison and made a monstrous attack on yet another German anti-aircraft emplacement, which I later learned was in the hilly Grebbe area. This time, all kinds of metal objects flew in the air. Then the Lightnings made a quick turn and took off at what must have been 700 kilometres an hour.

The Lightnings reminded me of our Dutch Fokker G-1 fighters, most of which were destroyed on the ground when the Germans attacked in May 1940. It was abundantly clear that the Lightning squadrons were now repeating the tactics the Germans used in their Blitzkrieg onslaughts at the beginning of the war.

Within an hour or so there was a lull in the mighty air circus, and it struck me that I was hungry. This reminded me that, battle or no battle, I should still feed the chickens. I bounded down the stairs and went straight out to the poultry. The poor animals were cowering at one end of the coop. They, too, were upset by the noise but still managed to keep up their interminably loud clucking. My heart went out to my normally productive little charges.

The chickens got a good feed from me and then I went inside hoping for a good feed for myself. The Bos family was gathered in the kitchen. They were in such a frenzy of excitement and fear they could hardly eat anything. My appetite was not affected, and while devouring a sandwich I tried to describe the beautiful, yet fearful circus performance above my head. In turn, they babbled back to me that they had seen two Allied fighter planes shot down and land near the house. We all managed to drink enormous amounts of ersatz coffee while we chattered. I doubted whether that would settle our nervous stomachs, but it helped to keep us alert.

Soon I heard aircraft buzzing overhead again. At the first thunderous crack I was back on the roof. I checked my watch; it was now a quarter past eleven and I could see the battle scene had changed. The planes were no longer over the Waal River to the south of us. The action had shifted to the northeast and I was pretty sure the planes were now over Arnhem and Wageningen. The anti-aircraft gunfire in the streets and orchards around us had virtually stopped, too, but the Germans were still ready and waiting to continue the fight. I looked hard and saw German soldiers crawling between foxholes on their knees. These troops were amazingly well camouflaged and could have been branches moving in a strong wind. The German experiences in Russia and Normandy had made them into superb soldiers.

My eyes were drawn to the sky again as a cloud of four-engined Lancaster and Halifax bombers appeared overhead. It was a display of power I knew the world had not yet seen. The sound was absolutely deafening. The sky had turned dark from this blanketing Armada of planes; I could no longer comprehend the enormity of what I was seeing. The earlier fighters had sounded like mice compared to the thunderous noise of the bombers. These behemoths were flying extremely low, perhaps thirty metres above my head. They were heading for Arnhem.

I was more than anxious about Uncle Carl. He lived across the Rhine, under their flight path. There must have been telepathy between us because half an hour later Mrs. Bos shouted up to me that he was on the phone. He had been concerned about my safety so had broken his rule of no contact. "The Germans are too busy to worry about checking the phones today, Fred. What's going on over there? Are you okay?"

I excitedly related all I had seen, and then it was his turn. He was full of news: The World Hotel had been bombed, the rest of that street levelled, and many had been killed. This famous hotel was only a few blocks from his house. He emphasized that the giant air attack was only the beginning and would probably last for days. From his contacts he had learned that part of the Allied mission was to secure four major bridges, including the one at Arnhem.

I rushed back to my roof-top perch. It seemed I had been gone for a lifetime, but only fifteen minutes had passed. More bombers flew by, still maintaining the huge Armada-like formations. I could see everything was still heading for north of the River Rhine, and we could now hear bombs exploding in the far distance.

Even before the last of the bombers had flown out of sight, I could see formations of strange planes in the distance. Each one appeared to be towing a big, square crate. The great mass moved forward in orderly groups of about one hundred and was now passing over my head. I glanced down to the street and saw farmers, heads upturned, staring at the sky. The strange phenomenon was mystifying to all of us. Strange or not, the planes were making new, even louder, straining engine sounds.

The minute I saw the cables between the crates and planes it flashed through my brain that the planes were towing gliders. I knew these gliders would be full of air-borne troops and equipment. Without thought I jumped up and down yelling, "Gliders! Invasion! Gliders! Invasion!" The farmers looked up at me. Then they too saw the cables and all became clear. One yelled, "Can you see any paratroopers jumping?"

The planes were now so close I could see the troops standing in the doorways. Some even waved to me. I silently prayed they would survive.

Later that afternoon, Uncle Carl called again. He wanted to give me the great news that thousands of paratroopers were being dropped on the edge of the Veluwe, an area north of the Rhine, between Arnhem in the east and Heelsum in the west. This meant there would soon be fighting on the ground.

The minute I was off the phone I rushed back to the roof. The clear blue skies provided a background to parachutes of every imaginable colour eerily floating downwards. On that auspicious first day of the battle, up to 8,000 British paratroopers would be dropped within my sight range on the area west of Arnhem. The American 101st Airborne Division released another 8,000 men at the Best Bridge, near Eindhoven, and the sister 82nd Division let drop some 7,000 soldiers at Nijmegen and Grave Bridges.

These 82nd boys covered the crucial river areas of the Waal and the Maas. My excitement knew no bounds. I jumped around the roof performing my own jubilation ballet interspersed with jaunts up and down the stairs. During one of these trips I ran full tilt into Mrs. Bos. We embraced, both wild with joy, then the others joined us and the embracing started all over again. Everyone was dancing madly around the room. All this celebrating was hard to resist, but after a while I went back to the roof. I didn't want to miss one shred of action and I soon began my wild jumping again. "Quit jumping so hard, Pieter," Mr. Bos shouted up the stairs, "you'll break through! Come down and have some more champagne"

There was a lot more hugging as we drank from the many bottles being passed around. We toasted the troops with every breath and wished them good luck in their coming fight. We had a feeling those guys could use as much good luck as we could wish them.

The evening brought a welcoming lull, although the light anti-aircraft artillery kept up its "ack-ack" noise in the distance. We could not forget only fifteen kilometres away the forces were shaping up for a huge ground battle. Outside the house, a few villagers were standing around discussing the day's events in quiet tones. The streets were empty except for the odd German staff car transporting captured English airmen.

Commentary

What little was left of the World Hotel was used later on May 5th, 1945, when the German General Blaskowitz surrendered to the Canadian General Charles Foulkes, ending the fighting in the Netherlands. Our Prince Bernhard was also on the scene.

Jaap Brakel, Fred's Opheusden friend in 1950

Hemmy van Milligen and Fred

A totally destroyed glider

93

CHAPTER 13

DAY TWO AND AFTERMATH

The lull continued the following morning and we were on tenterhooks not knowing what to expect next. Some of our neighbours were keeping busy building bomb shelters.

We would have been shocked to realize that the intensity of the German opposition on the previous day was to prove minimal compared to the assault on the second day. In fact, many of the German batteries had simply held their fire to conceal their presence.

It was the proverbial calm before the storm. All hell broke loose in the late morning when a mighty formation of Dakota aircraft daringly swarmed overhead. I could not imagine what pandemonium they were heading into. The German anti-aircraft guns responded almost immediately blazing away at the Dakota squadrons.

I got back to my roof station in time to see a Dakota directly above me get hit. A small lick of fire sprung from its fuselage and in seconds the plane became a fireball. Its great bulk spiralled mercilessly, over and over like a child's toy. It hit less than a kilometre away and burst apart with an explosion. It was engulfed by intense black smoke and I was transfixed watching what looked like straw spewing in the air. We who watched knew her crew had long since perished and were sick in our hearts; they never stood a chance.

On this second day, just as many gliders with men and supplies were coming in, heading for the landing sites. To my disbelief, the Germans were shooting down far more than they had the day before. There were more Germans, more guns, more hits. Planes and gliders fell out of the sky almost faster than I could count them. I started keeping track. In a period of twenty-eight minutes, I saw thirty-two go down. I had been so engrossed in my macabre count I had not noticed life on the roof was getting hotter by the minute. Anti-aircraft shell fragments and machine gun fire began ricocheting off the chimney. I left the roof in a hurry.

After a few minutes I was racing up the stairs again. I was no sooner up when I heard Mr. Bos yell up the stairs, "Look out for the glider heading for the orchard near Jaap's house."

The plane towing this glider had been hit, but the pilot had cut the cable between them to prevent both planes crashing down. I watched as, against all odds, the glider landed safely at the edge of the orchard right behind the Brakel's. Thirteen men climbed out and hid in the orchard. After what seemed like an age, I saw them reappear, run towards the house, and dive inside. I could only imagine the scene inside my friend's house.

I could barely contain my wonderment about the Allies landing all around me, and I was longing to find out what was happening at Jaap's. Of course I had to stay where I was. During the next few hours I experienced the terror of many more planes crashing down, accompanied by the sickening smell of burning oil, cordite and red hot metal. We tolerated these dreadful smells. However, we had trouble stomaching the stench of burning human flesh.

I became so mesmerized by all the action that I imagined I was at the movies watching a war film. The "screen" showed yet another murderous formation of transport planes flying by. The sound of their engines droning low over my head was amazingly real. I watched in a trance. A brilliant flash shocked me out of my reverie. A shell had hit a Dakota towing plane. A small plume of smoke shot out; at the same moment the glider was released to find its own way to earth.

Four men leapt out of the transport and I was greatly relieved to think these parachutists would escape the inevitable fiery crash of their plane. My relief ended quickly when a few seconds later it dawned on me the pilot was still in the plane. I could see he was trying to control his aircraft from turning over and over like a falling leaf. The tumbling was so violent it was a mystery that the wings stayed on his once-proud plane. There were shouts from below and I saw the neighbours had been watching this drama too. We all realized at the same instant the plane was on a spiralling course for the Bos roof — my roof. The villagers scattered, but there was nowhere for me to run.

I stayed stoically on the roof hypnotized by the shining comet hurtling towards me. Now that death was so close, I calmly accepted my fate. Squinting into the sun, I suddenly sensed the plane stop and hang in the air for a split second. I almost wet myself.

With a violent manoeuvre it wrenched itself level then pointed upwards, ascending higher and higher into the sky. One engine was providing this climbing power and the other, still burning, seemed primed to explode at any moment. The Dakota kept rearing upwards like a horse, when in a moment of surprise the pilot appeared and climbed onto the wing. Those of us left watching could see him clearly outlined by the ever-increasing flames. Then, dramatically, he leapt off the wing. I watched him until his chute opened, then lost sight of him. I also lost sight of the plane, but miraculously it reappeared quite a distance away. It was gliding towards the Rhenen Bridge, trailing smoke. I followed the plume and saw that the Dakota, which I had thought would be the end of me, now promised death to a German anti-aircraft battery by the bridge. The Germans fired like maniacs at the unmanned, burning monster, never quite realizing that they were the target. A great cloud of thick black smoke signalled that the plane had hit the battery dead centre. Not another shot was fired.

Talk about a hero! I could see the headlines, "Dakota pilot remains with wounded plane — Disengages glider — Tells crew to jump clear —Fights plane back to control — Masterfully sets it on glide to destroy enemy battery."

I would have given anything to meet this champion.

For the next few days I remained stationed on my high perch, but the action had moved off to the northeast. I didn't know at the time, but a fierce and bloody battle was being waged in the area between Heelsum and Arnhem.

There was very little news available to us Dutch citizens but it was rumoured the Arnhem battle was not going well. In fact, it was fast turning into a rout. It took a total of nine days for the Allies to lose their battle to conquer Arnhem and, in particular, its bridge.

The remnants of the 1st British Airborne Division were scattered; 2,400 escaped to the south shore of the Rhine, about 500 were hidden by the Dutch and some 1,500 were killed. The remaining 3,600 were taken prisoner, most of them injured.

On the south side of the Rhine, the British had captured the centre of Opheusden a few days earlier. This good news had heartened us, but we were now losing the fight to consolidate the earlier success. British armoured vehicles were being picked off individually by the Germans as they tried to traverse the exposed dikes. I was only about two kilometres from the Opheusden fighting, but it was now clear that the area where I was living would not be liberated.

We were crushed that we were still in enemy territory. The Bos family and I, along with several neighbours, sat around listlessly, consoling one another. Hour after hour and in the days that followed, I struggled to come to terms with the fact that I must continue to stay in hiding.

Finally, on September 20th, I decided to take my fate into my own hands; I must escape to the area the British had liberated in the centre of Opheusden. That meant going eastward through the orchards and ploughed fields that had now become No-Man's Land.

I knew it was suicide to attempt to cross that barren patch of land. The only way to avoid being shot was to convince the guards to turn a blind eye. I was well aware it was an enormous risk, but I was so desperate for freedom I decided to ask one of the guards to do exactly that.

The German soldier who was guarding the section of road near the Boses had been stationed there for some time. I had spoken to him often, so we had already become almost friendly. He didn't consider me much of a threat because I was just a boy, so he talked to me freely. He told me he was Austrian and had already fought in Normandy and the Falaise Gap, which had been hell holes for him. He was thoroughly fed up with the war, so I hoped he might feel some sympathy for me.

Cautiously, I told the Austrian I planned to escape. To my great relief he didn't march me off to his commander. Instead, he agreed to look the other way. I was so grateful I even asked if he would like to come with me. He declined, explaining that he dare not desert. Then I pleaded with him to warn the next machine gun operator, who was at least a hundred metres down the road, to hold his fire when I came through. I knew about this gunner, too; he was an ex-French Resistance man, a Maquis, who had been given the choice of a bullet or joining the German army. He willingly agreed to let me escape.

I trusted the word of the two men implicitly, enemies or not. The war and occupation had turned me into a rabid, German-hating boy, but these soldiers showed me that, one on one, the enemy could be human.

Jubilant, I rounded up Mr. and Mrs. Bos in the kitchen and excitely told them my plan. Mr. Bos blew up with his usual anger. He shook me violently, shouting, "You are only thirteen, what are you thinking of? I am responsible for you. I will not allow you to take such a gamble!"

To my surprise, Mrs. Bos joined the argument, screaming at her husband that they and their two children should join me in the escape. After much pleading, she won the day. Once persuaded, Johan Bos became enthusiastic about the venture. He immediately contacted his pastor, the Reverend Norel, whose home was in the already liberated hamlet of Hemmen.

The clergyman promised to house all of us — if we were lucky enough to get through.

Commentary

I continually observed that the clergy were unstintingly helpful to all citizens, and they maintained a strong support network for those in need. Johan Bos knew he could count on their pastor. It is often forgotten that Hitler and his henchmen, one way or another, killed millions of Christians who were against the totalitarian regime. This outrageous figure included many who had aided the oppressed. The Poles claim documented deaths of some three million Christians during the war.

The British troops I had seen running into the Brakel's place commandeered the house and told Jaap and his parents to find somewhere safer to live. The soldiers stayed holed up there for several days awaiting orders. The Tommies spent their time drinking tea and taking pot shots at the German troops as they travelled along the main road between Opheusden and Kesteren. Eventually the Germans blew up the lovely Bauhaus style residence, but the troops had long since fled. Through some reparation scheme of the British Government, the Brakels rebuilt a new house after the war, again in a beautiful, modern design. The scheme was so generous they even got new bicycles to replace the ones that the soldiers had made off with when escaping the area.

CHAPTER 14

FLIGHT THROUGH
NO-MAN'S LAND

On the morning of September 21ˢᵗ, 1944, the five of us ate a meagre breakfast and packed a small suitcase each. I told the Bos parents to take only the bare minimum because too much luggage would slow us down. So with great reluctance, I left behind the beautiful leather Bible Uncle Carl had given me. I was reminded I had already lost my children's Bible during the rapid departure from the chicken coop. I still hated the Germans, but in contrast I had developed into a quasi religious child, obviously influenced by the families who had hidden me. Furthermore I could not brush off the intensity of the Arnhem battle and the terrible slaughter I had just witnessed.

I had been under the stifling constraint of being in hiding twenty-seven months. Now that I was on the verge of regaining my freedom, I felt a flutter of excitement in my youthful spirit. It crossed my mind that having the Boses with me was a double-edged sword. Although it would be good to have company, and their connection to the Norels would certainly be a help to me, I was afraid they would slow me down. Also, a group of five running across that barren stretch of land would be more noticeable than one. Even though the venture would be riskier than I had bargained for, the thought of abandoning my plans never entered my head. Perhaps I had become immune to fear. Or perhaps I had forgotten that bullets have no mercy.

I was anxious about how the Austrian guard would react to the news he now had to give safe passage to five. At about nine, Mr. Bos and I ran down the garden to inform him, and to tell him we were about to leave. The Austrian took the news calmly and promised he would pass it on to the French guard. We returned to the house and nervously wheeled out four bikes loaded with our cases. Then we were on our way. Amazingly, none of us had the jitters; we were just anxious to get going. The first obstacle loomed ahead of us; the orchard fence. We climbed it quite easily, but dragging the bikes up after us was exhausting. Not daring to stop and rest, we moved away from the fence as soon as we could and began picking our way between the stark fruit trees.

The orchard section conquered, our group now faced 150 metres of open, deeply rutted land. We would be completely exposed. So far, both the Austrian and the Frenchman had kept their word and withheld fire. Just the same, we took our first few steps out into the open field with heart-thumping trepidation. At first, we walked slowly and carefully, but our steps soon quickened. Suddenly our resolve to stay calm broke and we burst into a fear-fuelled run. The five of us continually tripped and stumbled over the ploughed, shell-cratered ground, alternately pushing and pulling the bikes.

We were about half way across when we heard rapid machine gun fire from the direction of the ex-Marquis gunner. The fire was not aimed at us, but we instinctively flung ourselves into a ditch. We lay motionless listening to the Germans and Allies firing at each other across No-Man's Land.

Our hearts lurched when we heard hand grenades exploding among the saplings we were heading for. We had banked on the two-metre trees giving us protection, but now we wondered if they would be a death trap rather than a temporary haven. The firing from behind us continued, and the din got louder and louder.

We pressed ourselves closer into the cold, sticky clay and prayed. It dawned on me that even if we reached the Allied zone, we would still be in danger from the warring factions. My dark thoughts were short lived; an Allied rocket-firing Typhoon flew over our heads firing at targets way behind us. The German ground fire stopped instantly. Without hesitation, we leapt out of the ditch, grabbed our bikes and ran like mad dogs over the last eighty metres of rutted terrain. We were so absorbed in our arduous trek we didn't realize we had reached the Allied side. We concealed ourselves among the trees and tried to determine whether the land ahead was clear.

Johan and his wife were limp from exhaustion and shear fear, but the children and I were exhilarated from our sudden freedom. We had made it! It was at this point that it suddenly struck me I had left no message for Uncle

Carl about our attempt to reach the Allied lines. I was flooded with guilt at my thoughtlessness to a man who had done so much to help me survive. I forced myself to ignore my feelings for the time being and concentrate on our flight.

As we got our breath back, we could hear, and then saw, the Typhoon firing two more rockets at Kesteren. The German machine gunners half heartedly shot off a few more whizzing bullets but soon all fell silent again. We were glad these fearsome Typhoons were on our side.

There were no more signs of grenade fire, so as soon as Johan regained enough energy, we made our way to a paved country road. Our jubilation subsided slightly when we saw white tape draped along the edges of the road. This meant that the ditches were mined. We gingerly manoeuvred our bikes onto the road surface. Johan squeezed his son into the child seat of his bike and we started pedalling. I was reminded of my family exodus on May 10th, 1940, when we left Amersfoort for the Overveen safe house. In my mind's eye, I could see my sister sitting in the child seat of Father's bike. It all seemed so long ago.

After a kilometre or so I spotted the shape of a British helmet poking over a ditch. I also saw the end of a rifle — and it was aimed at us. I swore mightily as we jumped off our bikes and put our hands up. Then I yelled, in my best English accent, "We are civilians just escaped from the occupied zone." Luckily, the rifleman kept his British cool and didn't fire at us.

I wanted to show my gratitude to the English Tommy, even embrace him, but I merely wished him good morning. "You were damned lucky to make it across," he said with a grin. "Go on to the Opheusden village centre; a Dutch liaison officer will take care of you." These were sweet words to our ears.

I wondered if it occurred to the Tommy that it would be just as easy for a few Germans to sneak across No-Man's Land and come round the same corner we did in a surprise attack. I hoped it would never happen.

As we cycled along the road to the village, I looked around and realized there were many British soldiers hiding out in the nearby houses. I should not have been surprised, after all this area was still mighty close to the front line.

I studied Johan and Greta and their children as we pedalled. I think the adults and I were still in a mild state of shock after our ordeal, but Arie and Ella were standing up well. They were probably enjoying every moment of the escape and looked on it as a new adventure, as I had when I was whisked away to a hiding place for the first time.

The Dutch liaison major greeted us enthusiastically. We answered all his questions and I told him the exact position of the German 88mm field gun and the machine gun positions guarding the dike road. He was pleased with the information and told me I had a pretty good grasp of the war situation and battle operations. That was a great boost to my ego!

We told him we were heading for Hemmen village and he advised us to keep moving. "This is a very dangerous area," he said. "You'll be safer in Hemmen." He apologized for the lack of public or military transportation to take us the seven kilometres; we were on our own. "The road is constantly under German artillery fire but it's the only route out of this area," he explained. He then calmly arranged English tea and army biscuits for us. This was the only breather we'd had since leaving the Bos's house. Did we enjoy those cookies!

The major was right. We had no sooner left than we heard British artillery shells whizzing overhead. I was pretty sure the shells were en route to the German 88mm gun emplacement I had told the major about.

We kept cycling, continually diving into the roadside ditches when the shells got too close for comfort. We got efficient at hurling ourselves from the bikes and were thankful these ditches were not mined. The shells were being fired from a spot less than 500 metres away and were not at their height curve when overhead. We did not breathe easily.

Shells began coming from the opposite direction, too, and I speculated they were from the Germans stationed across the Rhine. We could not tell whose shells were whose, but then it didn't really matter. The dead cows in the fields along the road, their legs sticking straight up, did not care whose shells had killed them. I knew even then that the sight of those stiff legs would stay in my memory. Animals, too, pay the ultimate price in war time.

We couldn't wait for our harrowing cycle ride to end. I started wondering if we were crazy to attempt this journey in broad daylight. I had asked the major if we should travel under the cover of night, but he said German patrols were prowling throughout the night and shot at anything that moved.

Our brave little group finally reached Hemmen mid afternoon. We headed for the Norel residence, a massive old home. The Bos family, with me in tow, was received in a royal manner with truly open arms. I immediately called Mrs. Norel my first liberation mom.

She showed us around the house and assigned us bedrooms. I was to share a room with the children. She told us they spent much of the time in the cellar. Its walls were fifty centimetres thick, so it was the safest place to wait out the German artillery raids. We were all relieved when she said it would take a direct hit before the house would be seriously damaged. I puzzled over why the walls had been built so strongly, for surely nobody dreamed of the destructive shells that would rain down fifty years later. Perhaps it was divine intervention.

Only slowly did it dawn on our little group that we had really thrown off the German yoke, and that we could now relax. The adrenaline that had kept us going all day was ebbing. In its place we felt hunger, thirst, and numbing fatigue.

Mrs. Norel was determined to feed us well. She set a marvellous pre-war meal on her large oak table. There was roast chicken, homemade bread, farm butter, and a gorgeous apple pie. The Reverend Norel's brother, a well known author, joined us for the stupendous meal. I considered the pastor the perfect Lord's representative; he had good connections both high and low. The awesome meal went on and on and we all over ate. We finally fell into bed and slept soundly during our first night of freedom.

Within a few days I was out exploring the hamlet. Its only claim to fame was a pseudo castle, which actually was a splendid residence. I noticed that the British had not commandeered the lovely home.

There were hundreds of British troops in the area, living in tents, trucks, or in commandeered homes. The Bren gun carrier crews had pitched their tents in the grounds of an ancient church just north of the castle. I wandered among them and discovered they were a generous bunch, passing out cigarettes and cans of ham. It seemed to me they were never without a mug of very dark tea in their hands.

I enjoyed being with these British soldiers. They never seemed to stop laughing, even though shells were piercing and compressing the air above making devilish sounds. My natural reaction was to duck when I heard the whooshing noise, but the Tommies just kept drinking their tea. I soon learned to follow suit. Tough guy!

During those first few days of our stay in Hemmen, we craved news about the battle of Arnhem. We were oblivious of the fact that fighting was almost over by this time. When the shocking news did filter through, we learned that the British had lost an entire elite division in the struggle.

We ached to read a newspaper, but none were to be had yet. We even tried listening to Radio Orange on the BBC, but we quickly deduced inaccurate news was being broadcast to mislead or confuse the enemy. So we just sighed and bore the steady stream of German shell fire showering down around Hemmen. The Germans were only two kilometres away from the Norel house. We spent a lot of time in the basement during the next few weeks.

In early October, units of the famous 101st US Airborne Division arrived to help defend the area around Zetten-Hemmen. The Americans settled in and erected more tent camps, and soon some of the men were attending Reverend Norel's services. They were charmed by his small but fine old church.

I visited the American camps, too, and watched them dig huge foxholes in the damp clay. They manned heavy machine guns from these dugouts and also slept in them. They were large enough for several men to sleep, but were extremely cold. A sergeant told me they had each been given an army issue 100% wool blanket to help counteract the cold. I could not help noticing the American troops were certainly better equipped and fed than their British comrades. Some of the disgruntled British troops grumbled about this to me.

Despite the American presence, we continued to suffer daily shellfire. One bright day pandemonium broke loose. A rogue German Tiger tank with about 300 grenadier troops in its wake had broken through the battle line into Allied territory in the western Betuwe. It was heading across the muddy fields straight for our part of Hemmen. There was virtually no holding this steel monster, the most powerful tank in the war. Five hundred guns fired at the advancing tank and grenadiers, but the phalanx still edged forward to within 500 metres of Hemmen Castle. The tank cut a wide swath of destruction as it repeatedly fired its fearsome gun. In a last ditch effort, the Americans brought out their special steel-piercing shells. That did it! The behemoth's onslaught was over. The American Division had long feared this super heavy metal goliath, and the soldiers were overjoyed that they had finally destroyed the Tiger. The death toll was high; only fifteen German grenadiers were taken prisoner.

I liked the men of the 101st Airborne Division as well, and began visiting them daily at their different machine gun posts. They took to me, too, because I spoke English. Many of them shared their stories with me; I found them fascinating. Most had jumped on D-Day at the Cotentin peninsula. To my surprise one paratrooper had a Chihuahua miniature dog, which his New York mother had insisted he bring to keep him company. He couldn't stop talking about the dog, saying he fed it only meat, cookies and chocolate. He described jumping with the mutt inside his jacket pocket at the Normandy and Best drops. Dog and man had been taken prisoner in France. He had escaped, and here they were.

This guy, and many of the other paratroopers, sported a shaved head with one strip of hair running from front to back, Mohawk style. This had become a "badge" for many Allied paratroopers and they wore it with pride, claiming it made them more intimidating to the enemy.

A few of the paratroopers were convicts who had been given the chance to earn a pardon by joining an airborne division. They made damn good specialty troops. There were also many African American and Aboriginal paratroopers among the 101st .

The Boses and Norels joked they never worried about where I was because they could always find me chatting away with the paratroopers. At first, some of the guys seemed puzzled by my presence; they could not figure out why a young boy was virtually alone at the battle site away from his parents. Most were too polite to ask questions but I eventually told them my story.

It was strange being able to give my real name to anyone I came across. In fact, it felt as though I was lying. Ever since I had crossed to freedom I had been telling myself constantly, yes, you are Fred van Zuiden. The enormity of no longer being under Nazi racial stricture, and not having to be someone else, was only slowly sinking in. The Bos family, too, had to get used to calling me Fred van Zuiden.

The paratroopers showed great interest and warmth when I related the adventures at my many different hiding places. I enjoyed these instant friendships purely for friendship's sake, but there was an added reward. They generously shared their K-rations with me. Mrs. Norel was feeding us well but, being a teenager, I was always hungry.

Some of the guys gave me their American addresses, asking me to keep in touch after the war. It was rumoured the 101st Division would shortly return to France to recover from their efforts in Holland. A few of the more gregarious soldiers even invited me to join their unit in France over Christmas.

I went along with their camaraderie but I knew only too well their generous holiday invitations would come to nothing. Wartime travel was still fraught with problems, not to mention there were no trains or buses.

My visits to the American and British soldiers came to an abrupt end in November. The Dutch authorities decided to evacuate all civilians from the area because it was still so dangerous. Civilian casualties were rising daily.

Although I hated to leave my new friends, I knew it was time to go. We were all suffering from the stress of living under the almost constant heavy artillery fire. The family Bos and I packed our cases again and made sure our bikes were in good working order. Luckily, we would be able to take them with us.

Many of the evacuees were apprehensive about the coming journey. I didn't worry about it. Compared to our dash across No-Man's Land, it would be luxury travel.

Commentary

Many months after our escape from the occupied zone, I discovered that Uncle Carl had come to the Bos home looking for me soon after I left. He had crossed the Rhine River ferry under terribly dangerous conditions, and had cycled almost ten kilometres through the war zone. I imagined him dodging shells and mortar fire, and being deafened by the roar of planes overhead. I also imagined how worried he must have been when he found the house empty. He had risked his life to check up on me. How lucky I had been to have this man's protection. I was plagued with guilt over not leaving him a message.

After leaving the Hemmen area, my American 101st friends had a brief respite in Northern France, but they were not there during Christmas as they had hoped. By then they were embroiled in the Ardennes offensive and the fierce battle for Bastogne; their Christmas was not a joyous affair. This battle was the last World War II European theatre offensive by the German armed forces.

Hemmen castle was very much in sound shape when I was evacuated there. By the end of the war, it had been totally destroyed by military action. When I returned five years later, I could not believe a building could be so completely obliterated.

CHAPTER 15

EVACUATION

Dozens of British Bedford trucks rumbled into the village. Most of them were already filled with people from nearby Zetten, but there was still plenty of room for us in the large canvas-covered trucks. We were allowed minimal luggage but that didn't matter to me or the Bos family. We had little more than the clothes we had fled in, anyway. I marvelled at how many people the trucks could carry and at how courteous and friendly the British soldiers were as they helped us in. Numerous little problems arose, but our liberating Allies settled everything with aplomb.

As soon as the trucks started moving we were engulfed in exhaust fumes. None of us felt we could complain, even though our eyes watered and we coughed like crazy, so we just used our handkerchiefs as makeshift masks.

Once in a while the trucks stopped and we gratefully stretched our legs. One of the breaks was in Nijmegen. I stared at the heavily fought over bridge. Surprisingly, it had not been damaged badly. However, the rest of the ancient city had not been so lucky. I studied the mighty Waal River again. Despite the devastation on its banks, it still shone and showed us her stunning beauty.

One of the truck passengers told us that some time after the Nijmegen Bridge had been secured by the Allies, the Germans tried to sabotage it. Several former Olympic swimmers slipped into the river many kilometres upstream, with the intention of attaching explosives to its huge pylons. Luckily, Dutch guards saw the men as they swam close to the bridge and quickly captured them.

Most of the passengers got out of the trucks at Eindhoven, including the Bos family and the Norels. Sadly, there was no time for goodbyes in all the confusion. I went on to Geldrop, an area that had been liberated since September. We had been assigned billets, and our host families picked us up from the truck drop.

Once again, my path crossed with God fearing people. My hosts were Frits and Neeltje Schrey. They had a five-year-old adopted daughter, Minnie. This child had been orphaned when her mother, Neeltje's sister, was killed in a bombing raid. Grandma, an evacuee, also lived at the Schrey house.

Each member of the Schrey family gave me a hug and I felt safe and welcome. I sensed they were proud of their simple home. The house was clean and warm, with the bedrooms in the attic, and living area and kitchen spread across the main floor. There was even a Sunday best room.

Mr. Schrey showed me around outside. He pointed out the large open field across from the house and told me, "Field Marshall Montgomery often lands his Piper Cub there when he visits his secret headquarters." There were high-tension pylons near the landing field and it brought back an old memory of seeing a Piper Cub save itself from a diving Messerschmitt attack by continuously circling around a pylon.

He also showed me his vegetable garden and an area where he kept a few chickens. The garden had been so productive the family had piles of vegetables stored in a root cellar. The Schreys had survived easier than the town dwellers because of their garden and chickens.

Pretty soon after my arrival the Schreys were required to billet two officers from the British Supply Corps, each with a batman. Fortunately, the British Army supplied food for the officers and men. Despite the Schrey's garden, this extra food was a real bonus; the leftovers found their way to the rest of us.

I had not known until then that officers had personal servants called batmen. I had not known about British arrogance and class distinction, either. I was shocked when I saw the disdain with which the Captain treated me and the rest of the Schrey household. The Lieutenant had a slightly softer tone, and the two batmen were very cordial. I soon made friends with them, and they kept me enthralled with their tales of battle. They also often mentioned what wonderful fighters the Canadians were. I was sorry I had never been in an area where I could have met some of them, the way I had the British and Americans.

It so happened that both batmen bore the name Fred, so with Frits there were now four of us with the same name in the household. (Frits is another form of Fred.) We called ourselves The Four Freds. Fred Gammage had a very red nose and was about fifty. His colleague Fred Wren was in his mid twenties. Soon after they moved in, the younger Fred gave me an English army beret. I wore it proudly, pretending that I, too, was an English soldier.

The officers were given the Sunday best room. The hospitable Mr. and Mrs. Schrey moved their bed and Minnie's cot behind a curtain in the attic, leaving a bedroom for Fred Wren and me. Fred Gammage made claim to a folding cot in the living room, and Grandma was given the pull-down bed in an alcove off the kitchen. Thankfully, the house had been built with several sinks and W.Cs.

It was a great relief to be farther away from the frontline and out of the continual shell fire. However, the area was not tranquil. Allied planes droned overhead day and night, on their way to bomb German cities. Despite the turbulence still swirling around us, there was always a happy go lucky atmosphere at the Schrey home. I reckoned it came from the character of the southern Hollanders, who seemed to have a lighter outlook on life. I am quite sure the very decent, religiously inclined Schreys did not have a mean streak in them. There was loads of fun at mealtimes, especially when we were joined by the two Tommy batmen. The Britishers loved to joke about their arrogant officers quietly dining in a separate room. I honed my English translating all the repartee.

During that winter I spent a lot of time walking and cycling in the nearby countryside. I didn't have any chores to speak of, so made the most of my freedom. I cycled to Eindhoven several times to see the family Bos in their billeted home. We were good friends by now and were always happy to see one another.

One chilly day I was walking in the fields behind the Schrey home when I recognized the sound of a particular German plane overhead. I watched for a while and saw the Junker 52 drop a parachutist. I was now a seasoned little trooper of fourteen, and my military mind immediately suspected the parachutist might be a saboteur being dropped behind Allied lines. After all, Prince Bernhard and Montgomery had their headquarters in the area. I rushed home to get my bike and cycled to Geldrop because I knew the sighting would interest the military police there. They caught the man quickly and he proved to be a German-trained saboteur in civilian clothes. I never heard what happened, but he was likely shot under the War Rules.

Another of my forays led to an even more astonishing event. I was cycling to Eindhoven when I noticed two Dutch guards standing outside a villa. I asked them why they were there, and they told me they were on guard; this was Prince Bernhard's headquarters. The Prince headed the Princess Irene Brigade and was a member of the Military Authority ruling that part of liberated Holland. With youthful bravado, I asked for an audience with the Prince. I did not dream I would convince the guards, but one of them took me to the Prince's office immediately.

His Highness politely sat me down and asked why I had wanted to see him. In truth, I didn't really know, but I was soon telling him all about my war experiences. He listened closely. "I'm amazed at what you've gone through," he said, and asked me to repeat my account of how we had crossed No-Man's Land. While I poured out the story, the Prince's aide recorded the details.

Feeling confident that the Prince would now consider me as war hardened as I believed myself to be, I offered my services as a courier. I told him I was even prepared to return to the occupied and starving parts of Holland. The Prince looked at me quizzically then asked my age. When I said fourteen he rejected my offer in no uncertain terms. With my audience apparently at an end, he thanked me graciously and wished me good luck. I left the room walking on air and the aide escorted me to the front gate. Meeting the Prince was a great thrill, especially after the recent rocky years of my young life.

There was always plenty of hullabaloo around the Schrey home, including the dubious pleasure of listening to the German V-1 rockets flying over our heads. We sympathized with the British under fire from the rockets being shot from our west coast. We got the willies listening to the rockets' so-called "breathing problems" as they hesitated and got going again. There was not much we could do except sit around in a nervous state until the lethal missile passed by. We marvelled that each rocket could resume its journey considering all the spluttering it did. No doubt it continued in this fashion all the way to its final destination of Antwerp or Eindhoven. It was critical for the Germans to disrupt Antwerp, which by now had become the second most important port in the Allied re-supply line.

Ever since I had been with the Schreys, the Allies had been fighting a fierce battle in the Peel Brabant area east of us. The Allied mission was to clear the route into Germany. This was the heaviest fighting the Allies had been through since Normandy, and casualties were horrendous. At the height of the battle they were firing 60,000 shells an hour.

We were only thirty kilometres away from this fighting. We endured the dreadful sounds of battle and watched the illuminated night skies with a mixture of terror and fascination. We were thankful when the fighting ended on December 17 with an Allied victory. The Germans were in retreat!

Almost immediately after the victory Allied tanks began trundling by the Schrey house, heading east on the road to Germany. I counted about sixty tanks a day, plus troops and other heavy artillery and equipment. Then the flow stopped abruptly, and we were left to wonder what had happened. Later, we discovered that all forces had been redirected to the Belgian Ardennes to fight the battle of the Bulge.

On Christmas Day we tried to put this and other worries out of our minds. We gathered in the kitchen for a festive dinner and, to our surprise, the two officers asked to join us at the family table. For a few hours they did not pull rank and treated us as equals. We toasted one another, absent loved ones, and those still starving in the occupied parts of our country.

The Lieutenant even sang "Oh Jerusalem" in a magnificent baritone. His firm voice did not miss a note and our Christmas celebration became a truly heart warming event for each of us. The Schreys were particularly overcome, and I knew I was always going to associate the singing of "Oh Jerusalem" with Christmas. There must have been some subtle change in me that I quite naturally assumed I would survive to see future Christmases.

In early February, Sherman, Churchill and Cromwell tanks, as well as guns and troops in their thousands, again streamed past the Schrey's heading for Germany. By counting how many tanks went past each minute, then multiplying that by the hours they took to go by, Frits Schrey and I estimated that 300 tanks, and sometimes 400, went by each day. This went on for more than three weeks. We watched in awe and considered the tank columns our very own victory parade.

In January 1945, the Military Authority organized a system whereby Dutch survivors could enter their name in a book placed at every town hall in the liberated areas of Holland. The Canadian troops would then distribute the names to municipal offices in newly liberated areas across the country. It was an efficient scheme for relatives to learn of survivors. I eagerly set my name down at the Eindhoven Town Hall shortly after the system was established, praying that my family was still alive and that my father would see it.

During the next few months, many more areas of Holland were liberated. My hometown and the surrounding area had not yet been set free, but I knew it was only a matter of time. As much as I loved the Schreys, it was time for me to track down my own family.

Commentary

I rarely got to meet any Canadians because I was not in the south-west areas where they were fighting. However, they were our heroes; they fought for and liberated about eighty-five percent of Holland. Great Britain and the United States claimed the remaining fifteen percent. The Dutch are eternally grateful to them all.

Hitler invaded Russia, the then-Soviet Union, in June 1941 and created for the Allies an instant Comrade in Arms. The Germans encircled Leningrad and attacked Moscow that winter. They proceeded deeper and deeper into southern Russia with many victories. And then came the historic Battle of Stalingrad, which raged from July 1942 until the Russians claimed victory in February 1943. The Germans were seriously hampered by having to fight through two frigid Russian winters.

After Stalingrad the Russians consistently beat back the Germans until the final Russian victory in Berlin in 1945. One cannot dismiss the terrible losses suffered by both sides; the combined casualties at Stalingrad alone sit at around 1.5 million.

The overall World War II Russian casualties were high. Over four years of devastating warfare, Mother Russia lost close to 25 million of its people. In realty this means about 18,000 people per day. When I heard this statistic, I wondered how such a tragedy was possible.

With the nearing of the end of hostilities came the opening of the concentration camps, and every form of bestiality and inhumanity was revealed. Anyone who witnessed the death camp sites is forever haunted. How could a civilized country full of well educated and culturally rich citizens approve mechanized genocide? Perhaps it is a mystery that will remain for all time.

The huge infantry divisions and tank crews we had watched passing by the Schrey's house necessarily stopped en route for meals. Our prim Dutch sensibilities were a little bit shocked to see the awful mess of empty tins and garbage they left in their wake. However, we understood that liberating armies leave their detritus. We forgave them whole heartedly.

Frits and Neeltje Schrey, Fred's evacuation hosts

Fred wearing his British beret after the war

Three of the four Freds, Gammage, Wren and van Zuiden

Statue in memory of air raid victims

Statue honouring the Resistance

Chapter 16

Going Home

I left Geldrop at the end of April and set out on the first leg of my journey. I planned to take it in two stages. My first goal was to return to one of my former hiding places until my hometown was liberated. The Mettrops, Hendriksens, and Elizabeth Homestead were all in the general direction of my hometown, and so were the van Schuppens in Meu-Lunteren. They were my first choice because I felt Zwarte Gert, with his Resistance contacts, could find out about my family and the liberation of Hoogeveen, my hometown. I did not allow myself to think of the possibility that he would give me bad news. Nor did I allow myself to think of the possibility the van Schuppens might not be in Meu-Lunteren; they could have been arrested, or worse.

I had packed my belongings in a flour sack because my old suit case was not big enough. My clothes didn't take up much room at all, but my prized souvenir did; a five-pound British brass shell casing. My ambitious plan the first day was to tackle seventy-five kilometres to Nijmegen. I walked along the main road, looking back at the Schrey's every few minutes to wave, and began hitch hiking.

While waiting for my first ride I began feeling apprehensive about how I would fit in with my family after so long. What would we say to each other? Would we be shy? Would we be able to rebuild a life together? I pushed those thoughts from my mind; just getting enough rides to take me the 170 kilometres to the van Schuppens was enough to worry about. There was no public transport and very few private vehicles on the road, so I would have to rely on military vehicles.

I got lifts in several army trucks, but only for short distances. When a large Mack truck stopped, I eagerly leapt into the cab. It was hauling a Sherman tank on its long flatbed. I turned to the driver to say thanks and was amazed to see a young woman, a WAAF, perched behind the giant steering wheel. I sat by her side entranced as she chatted to me about the route she was taking to get to the German front line. That ride was over all too soon.

While standing by the road again, I got soaked through when a military truck went by, splashing me with muddy water from a puddle. The lunch Mrs. Schrey had packed for me was long gone, and I began to feel sorry for myself. I perked up when another military truck stopped after only a few minutes. This ride took me over the Grave-Maas Bridge into Nijmegen. I tried to imagine the huge battle at the Waal river crossing west of Nijmegen, the scene of so many American 82nd Airborne losses. I shivered with sorrow as I relived what those boys had gone through in their efforts to try to relieve the embattled Arnhem troops. Arnhem was only twenty kilometres up the road, but the Americans and British just had not been able to reach it.

I had a little money and hoped to buy food, but there was none for sale. I was hungry and tired so began looking for a bed for the night. When I saw signs to the Military Authority offices, I decided to ask them for help. One of the men gave me the address of the local rabbi, saying that was the best he could do for me. I wandered all over the place trying to find his home, but the effort was worth it.

The family welcomed me warmly. The first order was a steaming bath and food. My clothes were laundered and I spent the night in a heavenly bed. In the morning the Rabbi told me he had once met my uncle, and invited me to stay an extra night. It did me good to have this chance to recover from my first day's journey, not to mention spending a few more hours in that celestial bed.

I was back on the road the following day, and the heartfelt farewell of the morning soon sunk into the background. After an hour of trudging I reached the Waal River. I began crossing the bridge then stopped to really look at the magnificent structure. I once again felt my spirit mingle with the ghosts of those who had fought so hard to conquer this and other strategic bridges. I kept walking. There were no vehicles, no soldiers, and no civilians. The whole area seemed deserted; it felt eerie. My feet were hurting, my legs ached, and there was not a ride in sight. I walked another thirteen kilometres to Elst. Here, I saw not only one truck but a whole convoy coming towards me. Each truck was carrying coal and the very first one stopped. There was no room in the cab, but the driver motioned me to climb on top of the cargo. As grateful as I was for the ride, I silently cursed the black coal dust; it was quickly dirtying my freshly laundered clothes.

The driver told me proudly that I was riding on the first convoy bringing coal out of the Limburg mines. Industry in war-torn Holland had come to a halt. Amsterdam had no electricity. This load was headed for that famous city to help get its factories going again.

Approaching Arnhem I saw the most famous bridge of all, the one that came to be called "a bridge too far." I had tears in my eyes when I saw the once-proud structure lying forlornly in a tangled mess of iron on the river bottom. The army engineers had replaced it with a temporary Bailey bridge, but however useful, it seemed a sad substitute. Traffic was steadily creeping over the makeshift bridge, and my driver sighed with relief that his convoy was able to keep moving.

There were some forty trucks in our coal convoy and we all stopped together at an Arnhem site for a break. My driver gave me fifteen minutes to look around. Only then did I realize how badly Arnhem had suffered from the fierce fighting. On the north side of the bridge was nothing but rubble. The fine old Erasmus church was gone, as were so many other old buildings. In Velper Plein, the main city square, I saw a strange sight: a grand piano standing lonely and forsaken on the sidewalk. I felt compassion for the beautiful instrument and my imagination raced with a dozen scenarios of how it got there: An act of looting caught red handed? The owner trying to move the piano to safety? I wondered whether anyone had played a few bars of Rachmaninoff to a ghostly audience on the square.

I returned morosely to my coal truck and we took off. I bade the driver goodbye when we arrived at a certain crossroads. The convoy was heading west; the van Schuppens were farther north. I started walking, hoping to reach Meu-Lunteren that day. In the outskirts of a town called Apeldoorn, I passed an army unit and greeted a soldier who turned out to be a military rabbi. I asked for a slice of bread because I still had not been able to buy food and my stomach was twisting with hunger. He must have seen I was exhausted but he turned me down, giving no reason. I was shocked. It was the only unkind gesture I suffered from the liberating forces.

116

Disappointed, I continued my journey north, my flour sack getting heavier with each kilometre. Common sense told me to dump the casing. I stopped and let my head slump forward deep in thought, trying to decide whether or not to leave my beloved souvenir behind. A woman nearby innocently asked me if I was looking for money. I was so touchy I let off a string of swear words. The poor woman must have thought me mad. Against all reason, I decided to keep my memento; the casing stuck with me through thick and thin all the way home.

My path led mostly through dense woods until I reached the outskirts of Otterlo, where I discovered a burned out German 88mm artillery gun. I was stunned to see how much damage a flamethrower had done to this unit, now a heap of twisted metal. It unnerved me to see metal uniform buttons and swastika belt buckles, all that was left of the crew. The Canadian Forces had done a thorough job.

It was getting late and I had no strength to go on to Meu-Lunteren. I took a few moments to work up courage then turned in at the next farmhouse to ask whether I could stay the night. The farmer said, very agreeably, I could sleep in his haystack. He gave me a blanket and showed me the way. He left me with an invitation to come to the house in the morning. I had a wonderful, refreshing sleep even though I had gone to my straw bed ravenously hungry. These kindly Veluwe farmers let me bathe and then indulged me with a huge, nourishing breakfast. I luxuriated in their hospitality marvelling at how willingly these good, decent people opened their doors to a stranger.

The next day I walked the last twenty kilometres to Meu-Lunteren, all the time thinking what a variety of wonderful breakfasts I had been served on my travels. When I finally reached the house I let out an enormous sigh of relief. The van Schuppens, Zwarte Gert and Rosa were still there. Rosa's baby, now a toddler, hid shyly behind Gert's legs; I was clapped on the back and welcomed as a prodigal son.

They asked me a million questions and I was finding it hard to get the answer out before they asked me another one. But I had a burning question of my own. To my enormous relief, Gert had good news. A Resistance contact had recently told him that Father, Arjay, and Annemie were alive; they had just arrived home. The areas they had been hiding in, as well as our hometown district, had been liberated by the Canadians.

I longed to be able to contact Father, but the phone and postal services were not yet operating. Gert promised to get a message to my family telling them I would be starting my journey home once I had recovered from my last exhausting walk. As I sank into sleep that night, all I could think of was that it was a miracle the four of us had survived, and that Father's insistence that we go into hiding had been so right.

I had also bugged Gert about Uncle Carl and Klaas van Houten. He told me they were alive but had been eventually forced into hiding in a nearby town, Veenendaal. I was determined to see them as soon as I could. I was bitterly disappointed when Gert told me it might not be possible. Even though the area had been liberated, a Dutch Waffen SS Division still held Veenendaal. These turncoat Dutchmen were too afraid to surrender, knowing their fellow countrymen would want revenge. Gert figured as the Allies were already in the area, they would soon force this Division to give up. In the meantime, the SS guards would not let civilians into their enclave.

However, I was not prepared to wait any longer to see Uncle Carl and Klaas, so Gert and I hatched a plot. He speculated that the SS guards would allow the Dutch police into Veenendaal because the traitors were probably trying to ingratiate themselves with the new regime. His plan was to pass me off as a policeman. Gert knew several of the local police, so we went to the station and told them our plan. Knowing Gert's high standing in the Resistance I was not surprised when they agreed to lend me a uniform and papers. They even gave me a bike.

Early the next morning I dressed in the uniform and Gert and I prepared to drive to Veenendaal. Before we had finished breakfast, we heard a stunning announcement on Radio Orange: the German forces in the Netherlands had surrendered at Wageningen. All Holland was free! We just about went mad with joy. Our celebrations toned down a bit when we also heard that the SS Division in Veenendaal still refused to lay down their arms. I was meant to play the role of policeman that day.

Gert then drove me and the bike to within a kilometre of Veenendaal and I cycled off to the checkpoint on my own. I was shaking, but covered the fear with my usual air of bravado. I was afraid the SS men would immediately see through my disguise and throw me in a cell — or shoot me. I looked much older than my fourteen years, but I wasn't sure I looked old enough to be a policeman. They kept me waiting at the checkpoint, and I thought the game was up. The guards gave my papers an overly thorough inspection, but eventually waved me through. Phew!

It didn't take me long to find the little house harbouring my dear friends.

I did not often exhibit much sentimentality, but the minute I saw Uncle Carl and Klaas I hugged each of them tightly. When I eventually let them go I smothered Mrs. Van Houten with kisses. They, too, had heard the wonderful news of the Wageningen surrender, and they had gulped down many glasses of Bols already. I noticed they watered down my drinks!

I was still feeling guilty about not leaving word for Uncle Carl explaining our disappearance from the Bos house. Once our celebrating calmed down, I apologised to him. He immediately told me to stop worrying. He said he had been upset when he found the house empty, but neighbours told him we had merely disappeared one day, and to their knowledge we had not been arrested. From that he had put two and two together. "Fred, these things happen in war time," he said. "The only thing I care about is that you are alive and standing here in front of me."

The last time we had spoken was by telephone on the first day of the Arnhem battle, so we sat around eagerly sharing each other's adventures over the last seven months. I stayed overnight then began steeling myself for the ordeal of going out through the checkpoint again. But I never did have to face the SS guards. That morning, May 6th, a line of Canadian Sherman tanks had persuaded them to give up.

Uncle Carl's first response to the surrender was to recover his beloved 1939 Packard. Its inaugural journey was a quick trip to Meu-Lunteren, to take me back to the van Schuppens. There was some urgency for him to return to Veenendaal because he and Klaas were planning to go to Amsterdam for a meeting. They had been approached about transforming their secret underground newspaper, *Trouw* (Loyalty) into a national daily.

The following day as I sat around the radio with the van Schuppens, we heard the news we had all been waiting for. In the French city of Reims, the Germans had signed an unconditional surrender to the Allies. (A separate German surrender was granted to the Russians in Berlin two days later, on May 9th.) The war in Europe was over at last! The relief from fear came flooding out and we celebrated VE Day until the early hours of May 8th, the day the armistice came into effect. I was beginning to acquire a taste for Bols.

I intended to continue my journey home now that the war was over, but the van Schuppens insisted I stay longer. They said I would be foolish to start another long walk before I had completely regained my strength from the last trek. Also, they could see I was still trying to come to grips with what I would find at home.

My hometown had not been bombed, and I was grateful for that, but I was worried about what the years in hiding had done to Annemie, Arjay, and Father. I was also afraid of what they would think of me, hardly a child any more. Doubtless, the three years had changed us all.

I wondered if Father would have the strength to rebuild his business, which had been commandeered by a Dutch Nazi before we went into hiding. My other worry was seeing Uncle Willem and Aunt Eva again and facing their grief. Meta and Henny had never been far from my mind since the dreadful day they had been taken; returning to the van Schuppens had brought back vivid memories of the scene. I still held out a vague hope they had survived the camp, but I could not really believe it.

I was easily persuaded to stay a while longer in Meu-Lunteren.

During this period, Gert took me into the village. We stopped at a large, three-storied villa and went to a small, dank cell in the basement. It held six unshaven, hollow-eyed men. They were all terrified. They were the Dutch Commandant and guards from the Amersfoort concentration camp. I thought these men would have been completely dehumanized from all the death instigated under their hands on their fellow Dutchmen and the Russian prisoners. But, yes, they still had the capacity for fear.

Gert tapped my shoulder and handed me a club, saying, "Feel free to get even with the beasts; you will be protected by the guards." All the terror and angst of the last five long years flooded back to my mind, but I was not prepared to dehumanize myself by attacking the prisoners. I took a few seconds to mentally commiserate with the dead Jews, rail workers, Dutch citizens and Russians who had suffered at their hands. As I stood watching these animalized humans, Gert taunted, "Don't be a baby, just let them have it." I could not bring myself to do or say anything. We drove back to the van Schuppen home in utter silence.

Finally, I felt ready to go home. To my great pleasure, Gert arranged for a former Resistance officer to drive me all the way. I would not have to beg for rides or walk the last hundred kilometres.

The driver picked me up in a small vehicle and we started out on the main Amersfoort-Zwolle route passing by Putten. I had already heard about the terrible atrocity that had taken place in that town.

Local Resistance fighters had seized a German lieutenant. In retaliation, the area SS Commander decreed that all male inhabitants of Putten be arrested and the town burned down. To diffuse the situation the Resistance released the lieutenant. It made no difference. Six hundred men were rounded up and shipped to German concentration camps as hostages. Less than fifty returned at war's end. From then on, Putten was known as the village of black widows.

My journey home continued on a major highway and, again, I found it eerie that it was almost devoid of traffic. Five years of German occupation had brought this bustling nation to an absolute economic standstill. What traffic we did see consisted of convoys of the liberating Canadian Forces. The odd military police or speeding motorbike dispatch rider broke the monotony of these never ending trucks. There was still only one lane of traffic over the mighty IJssel River Bailey, but our waiting time to cross was less than fifteen minutes. A few other bridges had disappeared but they had all been replaced by the ubiquitous Bailey versions.

When we reached my home province I was happy to see that many towns and villages were still intact. I was moved when I noticed a great many drawn lace curtains; I knew these were the sign of grieving families. The Germans had rounded up and shot so many Dutch civilians, often with the treasonous support of their neighbours, I felt a day of reckoning had to come.

The driver dropped me off in front of my home and drove away. The scene was becoming more surreal with each passing moment. The store was still standing, but the windows were boarded up and it looked shabby. The same lace curtains hung at the upper floor living quarters, but I could see they were dirty and bedraggled. This did not look like the place I had carried in my memory. I could hardly believe I had ever lived here. It seemed like another lifetime.

The moment had to come. I took a deep breath and pressed the bell at the front door. I heard the automatic door release click, activated from upstairs. I strained to hear a familiar voice. Instead, an unknown voice said cheerfully, "I know who that is." I went in, leaped up the stairs to the living room and ran into a woman who introduced herself as Niesje Jonkman. Apparently, my father had hired her as a housekeeper.

I was crushed. No one was home. Niesje apologized, explaining my father was out on urgent business. I should not have felt so let down; they had no idea when I would arrive.

Niesje continued apologising for the family's absence, then went on to tell me what had happened to the store. It was literally a stinking mess when Father returned from hiding. The manager had torn down the partitions and fittings and sold them, leaving the place an empty shell. The Germans then turned it into a warehouse for military supplies. At some point the plumbing went wrong; the lavatories had been evacuating into the furnace room for months.

Eventually she brought me a glass of hot milk and left me to myself in the former Sunday best room. Thoroughly deflated I looked around the room. The china cabinets were missing and there was a sideboard and chair I had never seen before. I ambled around the room then looked out of the window. While looking down at the old canal that divided the village main street, I wondered if it still had its old brackish smell. I was so wound up when I arrived I had not noticed.

I stared at my reflection in the window. I saw a sallow-faced boy wearing an English army beret. I had worn it every day since Fred Wren had given it to me. It had become an integral part of my persona and was probably a security blanket, too. I suddenly thought of the Lieutenant singing Oh Jerusalem on Christmas Day.

My reverie was interrupted by the sound of heavy footsteps on the stairs. I recognised the sound immediately; it was my father. I heard Niesje shout something to him as he passed by the kitchen, then the door was flung open. I sprang forward to greet him, my heart in my mouth. In mid stride, he stopped and stared at me. I could see bewilderment in his eyes. Finally he spoke. Emphasizing each word, he said, "Yes! You are my son."

When we finally embraced, he almost cracked my ribs. I could smell the familiar stale cigarette smoke in his suit, and I almost laughed with relief.

I was home.

Commentary

When the war began, there were 207 Jews in Hoogeveen. Very few families in the area made the decision to go into hiding. Consequently they did not escape the systematic round ups of Jews, which started in late summer 1942. Perhaps people simply did not believe such awful things would happen to them. When peace returned to Hoogeveen, thirty-nine Jews emerged from hiding; only three came back from the camps.

Of the thirty-seven close relatives who hovered in the background of my childhood, only eighteen survived the war and the mass murders. I was stunned when I recently visited the Jewish Monument in Amsterdam and found our family name engraved almost 250 times. Probably not all were related to me, but it brought home how total families can evaporate. I cried when I looked closer at the ages of those who had disappeared. Many were babies, just a few months old; others were in their nineties. All those souls listed on the monument were denied the fruits of the hard won peace, but their spirits stay in my memory.

Putten was only one of many ruthless German retaliations. Soon after returning home, I learned of other reprisals in Holland, including an incident at De Woeste Hoeve. Here, 116 men were shot in revenge for ambushing a German general. Not content with 116 deaths, another 147 prisoners were taken out of various Gestapo prisons and shot in the same punishment. Terrible atrocities occurred in many other countries, particularly in Ukraine and Russia

Another of Hitler's shameful schemes was to expand his territories eastward. His dream, named *Drang nach Osten,* was to exterminate indigenous populations and clear great swaths of land in the Slavic countries of Eastern Europe. These prime farming areas would then be settled by land starved German farmers.

The German retreat in April 1945 freed up the Allied bomber crews, and many of them started dropping food parcels en masse to the starving population in Western Holland. We Dutch thought it exhilarating that Allied planes were now nourishing life instead of dealing out mass destruction.

The United Nations was formed to maintain the hard won peace. War's end also brought on a new set of hostilities in the great initiative to shed the yoke of Western colonizing powers, particularly in Africa and Asia.

The emergence of Russia and the United States as the major world powers at the end of the war sowed the seeds of the Cold War. This political struggle between the East and West lasted for more than 45 years.

EPILOGUE

After a brief period of awkwardness, we became a family again. We shared our stories, even laughing at some of the bizarre situations we encountered. Little sister Annemie had been moved ten times, but thankfully all her families had been kind and loving. Father and Arjay were fortunate in having only three hiding places, all with good people. Arjay told me when there was danger they hid in a narrow crawl space under the floorboards, often for days at a time, and he found it hard to endure.

We didn't forget the past, but we did our best not to let it ruin our future. Like most kids my sister and I were resilient and we adapted quickly to normal routine, but Annemie pined for her real mother. My brother had more difficulty and he was often plagued with black moods. Father threw himself into rebuilding the business. Within a few years he had remarried and had another son, Wim. His new wife was a fine woman and made him very happy.

We all grieved for Henny and Meta, and I missed my cousins terribly. I went back to Amersfoort in 1947 to live with my uncle and aunt while attending the Montessori school. Aunt Eva did not smile for the three years I was there. Her anguish was so great that one day she wondered aloud why I had survived, and not her daughters. I understood her sorrow. Uncle Willem struggled with the double burden of comforting Eva while dealing with his own heartache.

It took me four demanding years to complete my interrupted education. I went on to serve two apprenticeships in retail management and then began working for my father. During these years I stayed in touch with many of the people who had hidden me during the war. My hero, Carl Keuning, the man who orchestrated the hiding places, remained a friend and mentor to me until the day he died. I also spent much time with the Klaas van Houten family.

I worked enthusiastically at The Sun, but my ambitions for the family business did not sit well with my father. I think both of us were happy with my decision to immigrate to Canada in 1952. I immediately fell in love with the beauty and promise of the country. Eventually I settled in Calgary, married, and established a sailboat business. Life is good.

Throughout the war years, I saw much good and too much bad, and it was difficult for me to draw a balance sheet. I cannot glorify war, but I know it brings out the best as well as the worst in humankind. Many people endeared themselves to me. They asked for little and risked a lot, yet unhesitatingly took me into their homes.

The Allied soldiers who befriended me hailed from diverse countries. I never forgot they, too, were away from their families. This disparate bunch made it possible for the sane world to breathe freely again. As time passed, I appreciated even more the effort these men had made to help the occupied countries survive. I knew they would never forget their fighting years. The Dutch are particularly grateful to their Canadian liberators. These men are still grand heroes and remembered as if the war was yesterday.

It might seem surprising that I can still recall my war-time experiences, but they regularly come tumbling out of my mouth as though they happened last week. I worried that eventually the mists of time might consume the details; I wrote this book to preserve my memories and to honour the wonderful people who shared my path.

APPENDIX I

ARNHEM REFLECTIONS

I had never been particularly interested in the mechanics of war, nor could I claim to be a student of Sandhurst or Breda, but being on the scene at Arnhem as a boy generated a consuming interest in the famous Arnhem battle. After the war I read most of the books about the turbulent events and I certainly did not always agree with them.

Operation Market Garden was the name given to what was to be a grand push to shorten World War II, in fact to finish it before the end of 1944. It was mainly a British and American venture with a strong Polish contingent, which sought to secure Holland as the launching ground for the final attack into Germany. Field Marshall Viscount Bernard Montgomery, widely known as Monty, was the man in charge.

The plan's objective was to clear a path across the lower River Rhine by capturing the crucial bridges. Airborne troops would be dropped at Eindhoven, Nijmegen, Grave and Arnhem, while ground troops would advance from the south to support them.

In the initial planning stages of Market Garden it was Montgomery's idea, after Arnhem was secured, to head to Berlin. Eisenhower firmly rejected the idea and the Supreme Allied Commander had to remind Monty that, since the Normandy battle in the previous June, the Allies were suffering from huge manpower and equipment losses. Indeed, the airborne landings at Arnhem, Eindhoven and Nijmegen were forced to come in over two days, due to plane shortages. Monty then pursued a plan to attack the Ruhr Valley, Germany's industrial heartland. This time it was the British Prime Minister, Winston Churchill, who rejected Monty's plan. Churchill demanded instead that the Allies occupy and destroy the V1 and V2 rocket launch sites the Germans had set up in western Holland. At least 100 to 125 of these radio-controlled rockets were being propelled each day causing enormous harm to southeast England, including London. It was fortunate that a good few of the rockets malfunctioned over the North Sea or were destroyed by daredevil RAF fighter pilots during dangerous daylight attacks.

In my humble status as an uninformed onlooker, I had sensed right from the start that something had gone wrong with the huge battle plan that was unfolding. In later years, I was to lay the blame for the eventual failure of Market Garden at the Field Marshall's feet.

Montgomery acquired his fame in his North African campaigns against the respected German Field Marshall Erwin Rommel. It is my opinion that it was mostly circumstances that gave Monty his victories against the superbly trained German forces. Most importantly, Rommel suffered a shortage of materials because the RAF had bombed his supply ships. This was compounded by Rommel's critical lack of tanks due to Hitler having diverted the bulk of production to the Russian front. The German campaign was also weakened when Rommel was away from the front lines due to illness.

Little by little I learned more about Montgomery and my view of him was again tempered by his connection to the defeat of the test invasion of Dieppe in 1942. Monty's command in this theatre had had particularly disastrous consequences for the troops, eighty percent of whom were Canadians. Dieppe had high casualties and many prisoners of war were taken.

Furthermore, in Normandy Montgomery was associated with the failure to close the Falaise Gap, which enabled some 10,000 German forces to escape the noose set by the Allies. Many of these troops and their tanks wound up in Holland and lived to fight the Allies another day at Arnhem.

The strength and sense of purpose of the Allied Command was often coloured by the constant bickering between Monty and the American Supreme Allied Commander, General Dwight Eisenhower. These tensions had started earlier, even before the Normandy invasion of Europe. Surprisingly, Market Garden was little affected by this unpleasantness, except perhaps in matters of overall strategy. Eisenhower indicated his support for Market Garden by placing the American 82nd and 101st Airborne Divisions under Montgomery's command.

I have never understood why Supreme Commander Eisenhower, who had previously overruled Montgomery many times, did not thwart the Market Garden plans. Eisenhower must have forever regretted placing the American divisions under Montgomery's command when the Market Garden losses were tallied. At the same time I feel that it was a crucial mistake on Eisenhower's part to have made the gesture. The 82nd and 101st had already suffered stunning casualties in Normandy, and were now reeling from the losses in Holland. In one instance alone, General Ridgeway lost 500 precious trained paratroopers attempting to cross the mighty River Waal, west of Nijmegen.

Another decisive factor that permeated Market Garden was that the British ignored very visible evidence of German military strength in Holland. British Spitfire reconnaissance planes took photos of German tanks being refitted in the Arnhem area, but Montgomery's Headquarters failed to respond to the news, either from lack of knowledge of the photos or by dismissing the evidence. These tanks were from the crack 9th and 10th SS Panzer Divisions, which had escaped earlier from the Falaise Gap.

Although the principal function of Carl's and Klaas's Resistance group was to organize the hiding of Jews, they also served the vital role of gathering intelligence. A highly secret telephone in Klaas's office gave direct access to the Supreme Headquarters of the Allied Expeditionary Force (SHAEF) in Paris. In the weeks preceding Arnhem, Carl's Group had warned Paris that German armoured units were being refitted at Dieren. This equipment was only thirteen kilometres northeast of Arnhem. The danger was compounded when the refitted tanks were moved to a site right in Arnhem and hidden beneath trees. Within a few days, significant numbers of battle ready tanks had accumulated. Again the vital intelligence was ignored. In my opinion a few well placed bombs prior to Market Garden's start date would have destroyed this serious opposition, and the Allies would have had a fair chance of victory.

The failure of Monty's headquarters to act on the intelligence it received about the tanks was, in my view, a major reason, if not *the* reason, Arnhem failed.

Carl and Klaas made great use of the SHAEF phone line to Paris to pass on intelligence. In-depth information was continually delivered to them from all over Holland via couriers, most of whom were women. The innocent little phone sat on Klaas van Houten's desk at the plant, and the staff was led to believe it was for internal communication. The British inadvertently destroyed the SHAEF line when they bombed the Arnhem Bridge right after the fighting ceased. From then on these massive amounts of intelligence were transmitted directly to the Nijmegen battle sites from Klaas's home phone. Carl and Klaas were highly praised by General Eisenhower after the war, and it was rumoured their intelligence group was deemed the most productive in all of occupied Europe.

Carl often spoke to me of the harrowing problem in intelligence of determining who could be trusted. Earlier in the war a group of fifty-three Dutch officers had been trained in England by the then-Special Operations Executive (SOE). These candidates took intensive courses about weapons, ammunition, explosives, communications and money. Each was given a transmitter and schooled in codes. Most importantly, they were taught how to notify the SOE if they were compromised.

It proved disastrous when the German espionage service penetrated the activities of these Dutch agents. As each one of the elite group parachuted back into Holland they were caught at the drop site. The Germans forced the transmission codes from the hapless agents and made them telegraph useless information to the SOE. Incredibly, these messages were not checked for the correct compromise codes and the tragic drops continued. A handful of the agents came through the war, but most were incarcerated in the Mauthausen Camp and did not survive. The Germans referred to the bluffing operation as "Englandspiel" (the game against England), and were able to perpetuate the ruse for about two more years. An associate intelligence group of Carl's was named "Albrecht" in memory of one of the lost agents.

The credibility of all Dutch intelligence suffered as a result of this and other failures. The mistrust went so far that British troops heading for Arnhem were told by Montgomery's headquarters not to trust local Dutch intelligence. However, subsequent Dutch Intelligence personnel worked closely with the British MI-6 and were highly successful in their joint efforts.

Despite the early negativity, Major General R.E. Urquhart, Commander of the 1st British Airborne Division, could not speak highly enough of the Dutch Resistance intelligence provided to his officers, or the help given by local doctors and nurses. The citizenry was praised for their efforts in hiding shot down airmen. The American 82nd and 101st Divisions also proclaimed that their drops into Gelderland and North Brabant were saved from even heavier losses because of the good Dutch intelligence.

There was another startling incident. Market Garden officers involved in the drops were warned not to carry the complete battle plans, and specifically not in any one plane or glider. About an hour before battle commenced, an officer of the 1ˢᵗ British Airborne Division was shot down in the marshy Biesbos area near Rotterdam. This officer's briefcase held the plans for the entire Arnhem operation. The briefcase was found quickly and rushed to Field Marshall Model's headquarters. Model initially dismissed the plans as fake, but just the same he immediately planned strategy to thwart the Arnhem operation. He realized the British plans were genuine when he received intelligence from German troops holed out at Calais. They were observing numerous aircraft and gliders crossing the Channel in the general direction of Holland. Model promptly mounted intensive anti-aircraft opposition from the men, equipment, planes and refitted Panzer division tanks already sitting in Holland.

Due to the moving battle lines and lack of communications after the first day of Market Garden, a high proportion of the Allied re-supply material fell behind German frontlines. The British planes were hindered in their drops because they were under heavy attack from the unexpected anti-aircraft fire and Messerschmitt machine guns. The minute the British captured any land, they marked it with flares to signal a secure drop area. The battle lines were so fluid some of the previously marked drop areas fell back under German control, with the markers still in place. The huge Allied containers with desperately needed vital supplies significantly strengthened the German forces. It was not hard for me to add "lack of secure re-supply" to my list of factors leading to defeat at Arnhem.

The British tank forces moving northward to reinforce the Arnhem airborne drops were greatly hindered by the sudden need to replace the Wilhelmina Canal Bridge, unexpectedly destroyed by the Germans on the same day as the Allied drops. I deemed this delay another fatal blow to the Arnhem battle plans.

The Allies finally crossed the Rhine six months later, in March 1945, fifty kilometres east of Arnhem. It took 17,000 airborne troops, along with amphibious vehicles, to complete the task. It makes me think that perhaps insufficient troops were deployed at the three original Market Garden landing sites, where only 10,000 men were deployed for each landing.

It became clear that the Allies had vastly underestimated the number of German fighting planes and tanks already located in Holland. Neither was note taken of additional battle-ready tanks sitting to the east just over the enemy border. Most critically, there were high quotas of German troops recuperating in Holland from previous battles who were readily redeployed to the Market Garden operation.

As fall and winter 1944 approached, battles still raged in the Zeeland and Western Brabant areas of southern Holland. Both Canadian and British forces were being constantly hampered by the damp cold and the numerous waterways crisscrossing the Dutch landscape. At this late date the Germans were still capable of mounting terrific opposition. I find the German strength quite remarkable considering the energy they expended to block the Allies from reaching Arnhem.

It always intrigued me that Field Marshall Model had never destroyed the Waal Bridge at Nijmegen, which I think would have been an obvious move. A working bridge would be an advantage in any future Allied move north and west. I speculate that the Dutch Resistance might have intervened by cutting lines Model had set to detonate explosives to bring down the bridge. On the other hand, perhaps the Field Marshall was leaving himself an escape route.

It may be fanciful on my part, but had there been an Allied success at Arnhem, the Germans might have felt it necessary to retreat over the Afsluit Dike, a masterpiece of flood control engineering. I imagined a furtive night time retreat and then the full blown destruction of the dike, if only as spiteful retaliation against the Dutch people.

Sixty years later many still ask if Operation Market Garden was worth the effort. The major objectives were not achieved. The Netherlands were not liberated, the ground was not cleared for a march into northwest Germany, and the rocket sites on the west coast of Holland were not destroyed. But the Allies did liberate a great part of Southern Holland and were able to establish a foothold for future advances against the enemy.

The American movie *A Bridge Too Far*, which was based on Cornelius Ryan's book about the battle of Arnhem, very clearly illustrates many of the points I raise here about the Market Garden operation.

Appendix II

Speculation on Future Wars

I have been careful not to allow my war experiences to colour the rest of my life. Just the same I find myself interested in all things military and, I suspect, I think about past and present wars more than most people. It is not hard to prophecy that conflicts and genocide will continue to burden the world, as demonstrated by the more recent horrors in Sudan, Congo, Zimbabwe, Rwanda, and Srebrenica.

But the face of war is changing. We must now contend with nebulous, terror-prone extremists. Perhaps these are merely the reconnaissance activities for larger conflicts brewing on the horizon. There are already hints that Middle East confrontations could escalate into a world war.

I speculate that future wars will be between continents or between the Western Christian civilization and the Eastern Muslim world. Perhaps Russia will join the West, and China will do the same. It is hard to determine what course African nations might take. Some of the southern Mediterranean rim countries have succumbed to the Muslim extremist world. I would hope there will be pockets of Western support in India, Pakistan, South Korea, the Philippines and Indonesia, although some of these countries have seen Muslim terrorism rear its ugly head. I dearly want to believe that most of South America would join the West, despite its few rogue leaders.

I envision that chemical and biological attacks would be the new terrorist weapons of choice. The world has seen the destruction caused by atomic bombs and somehow I do not see their future use. I do believe we should worry about North Korea and Iran, or any other countries developing atomic bombs. My mind runs back to the gas threat in World War II, which was never implemented. Only the concentration camps made use of gas in their killing chambers. I hope that the nations with terrible weapons will decline to use them for fear of retaliation.

There are other scenarios I could dream up, which would be a threat to the good life many of us live now. Our civilization simply cannot afford more madmen of the ilk of Stalin, Hitler, or Idi Amin preparing for aggression and mass murder, virtually undisturbed. It is hard to speculate what propaganda such men would feed us to justify their ambitious plans, but the age old issues of race, religion and politics will likely not go away. Perhaps the lack of water will soon be added to the list.

Will we see a new drummer come along to tell us it is time to stand up again to prevent the destruction of our halfway-decent world?

Will the heads of the western nations earn back the favour and support of their peoples, so that we can join together to ward off any threats to the world's stability?

How the Germans must have been encouraged, when the Allies watched placidly as the Germans grabbed the Sudetenland, seized back the Rhine Land, and annexed Austria. Where were the protests when the Italians declared war on the almost primitive Abyssinians? Great Britain and France did not wake up and declare war on Germany until the Germans attacked Poland on September 1, 1939. By then it was too late.

Appendix III

Tables and maps

I have provided the table and maps on the following pages to help readers keep track of the many places I stayed at between leaving my uncle's home in Amersfoort in July 1942 and returning to my own home in Hoogeveen in May 1945.

Departed Amersfoort on July 20, 1942				
Dates	Location	Host	Length of Stay	Chapter
July 1942	Amersfoort	van der Pol	Stopover	4
July	Terschuur	van der Born	Short-term	4
July - August	Terschuur	Janssen	Long-term	4
August - November	Voorthuizen	Dr. Mettrop	Long-term	4
November	Wageningen	Uncle Carl	Short-term	5
November 1942 to July 1943	Lunteren	Elisabeth Homestead	Long-term	6
July - August	Meu-Lunteren	van Schuppen	Long-term	7
August	Meu-Lunteren	The farmer	Stop over	7
August 1943 to January 1944	Meu-Lunteren	Hendriksen	Long-term	9
January	Lunteren	The storekeeper	Stopover	9
January	Wageningen	Uncle Carl	Short-term	9
January - March	Heelsum	Jansen	Long-term	10
March	Wolfheze	Forest Warden	Stopover	10
March	Wageningen	Uncle Carl	Short-term	10
April - May	Heelsum	van Milligan	Long-term	11
May	Heelsum	The dentist	Stopover	11
May	Heelsum	van Milligan	Long-term	11
June	Zetten	Parlevliet	Long-term	11
June - September	Opheusden	Bos & Brakel	Long-term	11, 12, 13
September – October (**Start of liberation**)	Hemmen	Rev. Norel	Long-term	14
November 1944 to April 1945	Geldrop	Schrey	Long-term	15
May (**Journey Home**)	Nijmegen	The Rabbi	Short-term	16
May	Otterlo	Veluwe farmer	Stopover	16
May	Meu-Lunteren	van Schuppen	Long-term	16
May	Veenendaal	Carl & Klaas	Short-term	16
May	Meu-Lunteren	van Schuppen	Short-term	16
Arrived Hoogeveen on May 14, 1945				

Stopover: Less than a day

Short-term: One to seven days

Long-term: One week and longer

Map of Holland showing my movements in the Gelderland Region

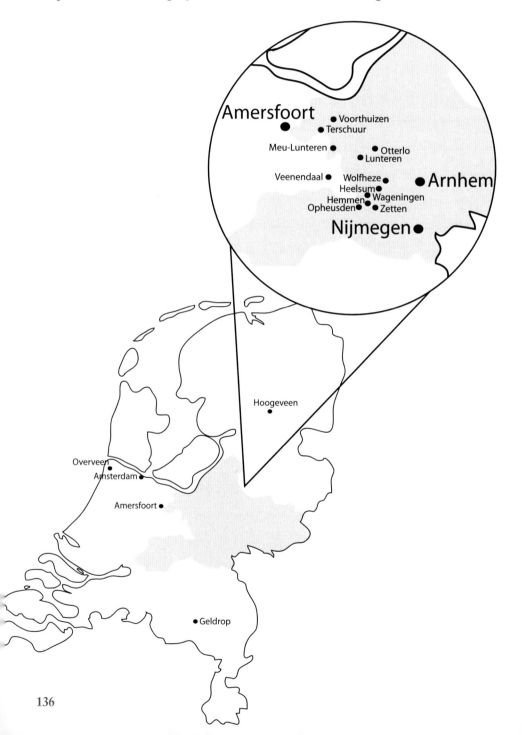

BIBLIOGRAPHY

Bloemendal, Hans (prefaced by). *In Memoriam:Le-Zekher,* Sdu Uitgeberij, 1995.

De Hess, Max. *Land Loopt Niet Weg:Drie eeuwen Joods social-economisch leven in Hoogeveen* (Land Does Not Go Away: Three Centuries of Jewish Social/ Economic life in Hoogeveen). Reestmond Druk, 1994.

Churchill, Winston. *Memoires Over de Tweede Wereldoorlog 1939-1945:* Volumes 1-10 (Memories of the Second World War 1939-1945: Volumes 1-10). Uitgeversmaatschappij Elsevier, 1954.

Churchill, Winston S. *The Second World War: Triumph and Tragedy,* Book One:*The Tide of Victory & Book Two: The Iron Curtain.* Houghton Mifflin/The Riverside Press, 1953.

Delilio, G.S.*W. Arnhem: Defeat and Glory: A Miniaturist Perspective of the Arnhem Battle.* Schiffer Military History, 2002.

Flim, Bert Jan. *Omdat Hun Hart Sprak: Geschiedenis van de Georganiseerde Hulp aan Joodse Kinderen in* Nederland, *1942-1945 (*Because Their Hearts Spoke: History of Organized Assistance to Jewish Children in the Netherlands, 1942-1945). Uitgeverij Kok, 1997.

Gunnink, G. *De KnokPloeg: Schimmen uit het verleden* (The Strike Crew: Ghosts from the past). Boom courantenuitgeverij, 2006.

Harclerode, Peter. *Wings of War: Airborne Warfare 1918-1945*. Cassell, 2005.

Harclerode, Peter. *Arnhem: A Tragedy of Errors*. Caxton Editions, Caxton Publishing Group, 2000.

Snyder, Louis A. *De Oorlog: de geschiedenis van de jaren 1939/1945* (The War: History of the years 1939/1945). N.V.Koninklijke Uitgevrij Erven J.J. Tijl, 1960.

Spring, Debbie. *The Righteous Smuggler: A Holocaust Remembrance Book for Young Readers*. Second Story Press, 2006.

Tjepkema, Almar and Walvis, Jaap. *Ondergedoken: Het ondergrondse leven in Nederland tijdens de Tweede Wereldoorlog* (Undergrounders: Underground life in the Netherlands during the Second World War). De Haan 1985.

Urquhart, R.E. *Arnhem: The greatest airborne assault of World War II – the battle for the Lower Rhine, September* 1944. W.W. Norton & Company, Inc, 1958.

Van Houten, Theodore. *Er Komt Een Andere Tijd: Oorlogsherinneringen van Klaas van Houten, Opgetekend door Theodore van Houten* (Another Time Will Come: War memories of Klaas van Houten written with Theodore van Houten). Refer Dr. C. A. Van Houten, 1993.

Werkman, Evert. *Ik Neem het Niet: Hoogtepunten uit het Verzet 1940/1945. Een keuze door Evert Werkman* (I won't Take It. High points out of the Resistance. A choice by Evert Werkman). A.W. Sijthoff's Drukkerijbedrijf,1965.

Acknowledgements

I wish to acknowledge the inspiration and wise counsel received from my editor, Pat Kozak, and the constant support rendered by my dear wife. I would also like to thank my brother Wim van Zuiden and my sister Annemie for helping with my research.

Thanks also go to the authors listed in the Bibliography. Finally, I want to congratulate the editors at Wikipedia for compiling information on the most obscure events.

About the Author

Fred van Zuiden immigrated to Canada in 1952 from his native Holland. After working in major cities from coast to coast, he settled in Calgary. He and his wife still ski and hike in their beloved Rocky Mountains, and Fred continues to compete in sailing events.

Fred is also the author of *The Sailing Game: Life in the Sailboat World*, a book about the challenges of running a sailboat business.